APPALACHIAN INDIANS OF THE WARRIOR MOUNTAINS

APPALACHIAN INDIANS OF THE

WARRIOR MOUNTAINS

by

Rickey Butch Walker

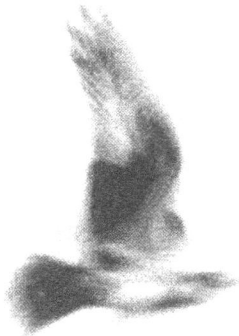

Published by:
Bluewater Publications
1812 CR 111
Killen, Alabama 35645
www.BluewaterPublications.com

Also By Rickey Butch Walker

Warrior Mountains Indian Heritage - Teacher's Edition,
ISBN 978-1-934610-27-5, $39.95

Warrior Mountains Indian Heritage Student Edition,
ISBN 978-1-934610-66-4, $24.95

Warrior Mountains Folklore,
ISBN 978-1-934610-65-7, $24.95

Doublehead: Last Chickamauga Cherokee Chief,
ISBN 978-1-934610-67-1, $19.95

Chickasaw Chief George Colbert: His Family and His Country,
ISBN 978-1-934610-71-8, $19.95

Pending in Publication

Appalachian Indian Trails of the Chickamauga

Celtic Indian Boy of Appalachia

Works in Progress

Black Folk Tales of Appalachia

Soldiers Wife: Cotton Fields to Berlin and Tripoli

When Cotton Was King of the South

Forward

Rickey Butch Walker, a lifelong native son of the Warrior Mountains of north Alabama, descends from Scots Irish, Cherokee, and Creek ancestry; he is a member of the Echota Cherokee Tribe in Alabama. He was born and raised in the shadow of Brushy Mountain, nourished by the subsistence of West Flint Creek and surrounding hardwood bottoms, and molded from travels of trails and paths wandering the numerous ridges and valleys of the great Tennessee divide.

When he was a young boy, he explored the wild canyons, hills and hollows of the Warrior Mountains. His Grandpa taught him to hunt various roots including ginseng, trap fur bearing animals, and stalk wild game from Indian creek to Indian Tomb Hollow. He grew up with a fierce love for the mountains in which his ancestors lived, died and are buried.

Walker has a post graduate degree in biology, education and supervision; he worked some 35 years for the Lawrence County School System. He eventually became the director of the Indian Education Program and Oakville Indian Mounds Park and Museum in Lawrence County which has become a model for other Indian programs nationally. In 1995 under his direction, the Lawrence County Indian Program was the US Department of Education's National showcase project.

Through Butch's vision of preserving our local Indian culture, he has helped save and protect our Indian heritage through his writings and advocacy for Indian people. Walker has teamed with friend Lamar Marshall to bring additional educational and cultural materials to our local Indian children.

Appalachia Indians of the Warrior Mountains is a cooperative effort of the writings of Butch Walker and the formatting skills of Lamar Marshall. We sincerely hope that the book will inspire as well as educate the young Indian people. According to Marshall, "it is clear

Lamar Marshall

that our link to the future is bound to our cultural links to the past. We must strive not only to preserve our natural heritage, but our cultural and historical heritage as well."

Table Of Contents

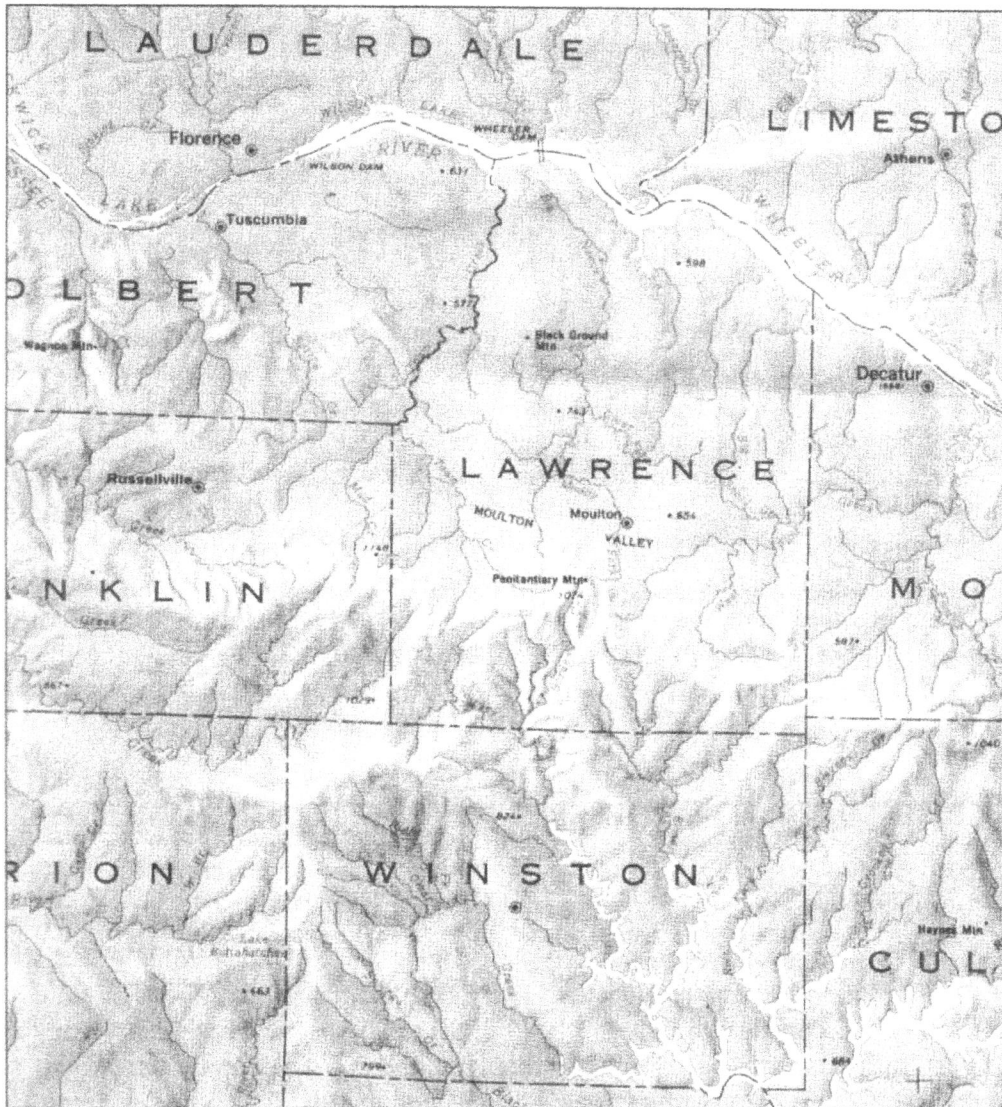

THE WARRIOR MOUNTAINS
OF NORTH ALABAMA

APPALACHIAN INDIANS OF THE WARRIOR MOUNTAINS

INTRODUCTION

Indians of the Warrior Mountains and the students of Indian heritage need an understanding of the origin, culture, plight of our Native American ancestors, whose blood, though diluted, still flows through our veins. The origin of our natives in the Warrior Mountains probably began over 14,000 years ago; however, it is generally accepted that some 40,000 years ago, small groups of hunters and their families migrated from the Asian continent across Beringia-a no longer existent Bering Strait land bridge into North America. By the end of the last ice age 12,000-14,000 years ago, nomadic hunters migrated throughout the continental United States, and became well established in our area of North Alabama. These early American nomads have come to be known as Paleo-Indians. Modern Indians of the Warrior Mountains are descendants of the Paleo-people.

Prehistoric Indians of the Warrior Mountains

Paleo lifestyle of the Warrior Mountains

The Paleo-Indians usually traveled and lived in small bands (Chapman 1985). Typical bands probably consisted of 20 to 25 people which were generally related. Both men and woman within the band had particular jobs. Men were responsible for the preparation of tools and weapons as well as hunting. Women were responsible for child care, crafts, and cooking.

The Paleo- Indians did not live in permanent settlements, but were nomadic and moved from camp to camp. Data from archaeological studies and the antiquity of Paleo artifacts indicate campsites from the Warrior Mountains to the Tennessee prior to 12,000 years ago. The locations of these camps were determined by the availability of animals, their primary source of food. Natural shelters such as caves and bluffs were used in addition to lean-tos and skin tents.

The Paleo- Indians are commonly known as big game hunters. The animals they hunted included: mammoths, mastodons, wild horses, camels, giant ground sloths, saber-toothed tigers, large straight horned bison, rhinoceroses, and deer. Most of these paleo-animals are now extinct (Lewis and Kneberg 1958) (Vogel, 1982).

The mammoths and mastodons were large (6-13 feet high) furry elephants that became extinct between 10,000-12,000 years ago. A large mastodon tooth can be seen in the Oakville Indian Mounds Museum. The tooth came from the area between Red Bay, Alabama and Tupelo, Mississippi. The mammoths and mastodons were examples of two huge prehistoric animals the Paleo-hunters utilized as a food source.

Some think these early hunters may have been responsible for a number of extinctions now known as the Pleistocene overkill; others attribute the extinctions of Paleo animals to changing climate and food availability. Mammoths and mastodons were herd animals requiring vast grasslands; therefore, herds in this area may have been small (Chapman, 1985). The Paleo-Indians hunted these large animals by driving them into traps, over cliffs, or into enclosures (Vogel, 1982).

Some planning had to be made before the kill took place. Because these were huge animals, there had to be a plan leader. Probably some members of the hunting party distracted the animal while others attacked the animal with their weapons. Because of the lack of transport and refrigeration, the animal had to be butchered on the spot and often eaten raw. After the mammoth/mastodon was killed, all parts of the animal were used. Brains and bone marrow were eaten. Brains were used in curing the skins for use as clothing (Wimberly, 1980). Although the Paleo-Indians are commonly recognized as big game hunters, they also included a wide variety of plant and animal foods in the diet.

Clovis Point from the Paleo period

Evidence of religious activity among the Paleo-Indians has not been found. The Paleo-Indian hunters used spears, snares, pitfalls, and other methods to immobilize the big and dangerous game they pursued (Vogel, 1982). A number of tools belonging to the Paleo-Indians have been found. These tools provide clues about their way of life (Lewis and Kneberg, 1958). The beautiful projectile points are given names such as Clovis, Quad, Folsom, Beaver Lake, Wheeler Triangular, or Dalton, after the sites where they were found. The points were usually thinned at the base, with many having fluted sides and ground bases. Daltons are commonly found throughout the area of the Warrior Mountains.

Many local collectors have paleo artifacts in their possession which came from areas within sight of the Warrior Mountains.

Stone tools served as spear tips, knives and scrapers when they were attached to small handles. These stone tools also were used to kill game animals, to cut up the meat, and to prepare the hides. Paleo-Indian pointed and flaked tools have been found in North America; however, more of these distinctive stone points have been found Alabama than in the entire western half of the country (Vogel, 1982). The projectile points were carefully made from thin, flat blades of flint or similar stone.

Illustration by Louis Glanzman, Courtesy of U.S. National Park Service.

First, a flat surface was produced on a nodule of stone. Next, a sharp and well-directed blow to the edge of the flat striking platform knocked off flakes that were long and narrow. These flakes were often ready to use as knives because the edges were already sharp. Other flakes were chipped of retouched to produce a sharp edge; those tools which were chipped on one surface only were called "uniface" tools (Louis and Kneberg, 1958). These one faced tools are very characteristic and distinctive of paleo craftsmen.

The scrapers were made by chipping a steep cutting edge along the side or at the end of the blade. A common scraper used to prepare hides, was usually trapezoidal in shape with the broadest edge forming the bit; occasionally, however, the bit ended in sharp spurs. Tools with spurs were probably used to slit the hides into usable sections as well as for engraving decorations. Scrapers were probably used in working wood, bone, and antler. The gravers were tools of small flakes with one or more finely chipped delicate points. The gravers may have been used for engraving. Gravers were also used for punching small holes in skins to allow them to be laced together to make clothing and other equipment. Other tools that have been found include rough chopping blades as well as flint drills used for boring holes in the wood, bone, and antler (Lewis and Kneberg, 1958). The Paleo-Indians had no known stone or ceramic vessels, but probably had baskets (Vogel, 1982).

Many paleo sites have been identified in the Warrior Mountains of north Alabama, as evidence by the tools left behind. The author has found or observed many Paleo artifacts from Poplar Log Cove in eastern Lawrence County to Mt. Hope area of the western portion of the Warrior Mountains. In addition, between the mountains and the Tennessee River are numerous Paleo artifacts. Paleo campsites have been found along the Tennessee River and along the major tributaries of Flint, Big Nance, and Town Creeks. Many major springs were the location of paleo campsites.

Probably the oldest Paleo artifact of Lawrence County was a Folsom Point which came from the Big Head Spring at the upper end of Spring Creek. The point was found during the Wheeler Basin studies in the 1930's. The paleo stone tools and implements have weathered to a white or light gray color which is evidence of extreme age. These Paleo artifacts usually contain a black or dark interior color with a white outer surface due to the extreme length of time being exposed to the elements.

The Archaic Lifestyle of
The Warrior Mountains

The Paleo-Indians, who succeeded in adapting to the environmental changes that took place at the close of the Ice Age, continued to live as a group archaeologists called Archaic Indians. A gradual warming trend occurred which resulted in the slow northward recession of massive mile thick ice sheets. Plant and animal populations gradually changed. Wooly mammoths and mastodons migrated northward and eventually became extinct. Archaic Indians were forced to adapt to new and changing food sources which led a gradual shift from the nomadic hunter society. Descendants of the Paleo-Indians were placed in what archaeologists called the Archaic Period.

The Archaic culture changed through diffusion and borrowing. The Archaic Indians lifestyle was based on the hunting and gathering of naturally occurring food and became specialized in the use of natural resources. Unlike their nomadic predecessors, Archaic Indians wandered within a restricted area. They maintained a home base or semi-permanent settlements. Homes were located along creeks and rivers during the summer. The river groups moved to caves or rock shelters during autumn before the winter floods.

Long term camps were established as caves and bluffs, large freshwater springs, and areas containing an abundance of food. The location of the camp was important. Camps were located at the sites of important rock quarries where flint (chert) was worked into tools. Camps were located where the gaps in the hills were found so that moving game would be concentrated. Homes were located along the shoals where spawning fish could be netted or trapped, and mussels were plentiful. Sites such as these are found throughout north Alabama and provided ideal camps; some of which were utilized over thousands of years from Paleo to the Mississippian Period.

Although the Archaic Indians continued to hunt, they no longer hunted large Ice Age animals for food; thus, their diet included new foods. The largest game animals hunted by the Archaic Indians were the elk and bear (Lewis and Kneberg, 1958). Other meats included deer, rabbit, squirrel, wild turkeys, fish, mussel, and grub worms. Deer was the most important game animal. In several of the sites, 90% of the bones were deer. In the fall, Archaic Indians gathered nuts, berries, seeds, roots, and other plants. Acorns became an important food. Ground acorns flour was made palatable by a process called leaching-trickling boiling water through the grounded meal until the bitter tannic acid was removed.

The change of the emphasis from butchering and processing of big game led to smaller game, and the harvesting of natural foods led to the new methods of preparing food. Nuts were cracked and picked. Seeds and roots were ground. Bark was beaten for fiber. Mussels were slowly roasted in pits with heated rocks. Stone boiling was a common process for cooking food. Containers of rawhide,

The Atlatl allowed the hunter of the Archaic period to throw spears with great force.

wood, or tightly woven baskets filled with food and water were placed into a hole dug in the ground. The water in such containers was then heated to the boiling point by dropping in hot rocks. Fireplaces were bowl shaped depressions scooped out for temporary use. Nut stones were used for cracking nuts. Mortars and pestles were used for grinding seeds and other foods. Many of these archaic remains are still found throughout the Warrior Mountains to the Tennessee River.

There is evidence of a form of religion among the Archaic Indians. The Archaic Indians had a medicine man that used the pipe and smoke to cure illness. The medicine man was believed to be a direct link to the Great Spirit. The ritual burial (the body buried with ornaments, intimate possessions, and pets) indicate a form of religion.

Archaic settlements possessed a common burial ground. The Archaic Indians were careful in the treatment of their dead implying emotions of strong affections as well as a belief in an afterlife. The arms and legs of the corpse were tightly folded against the body and were carefully bound in place. About one third of the burials were accompanied by such things as red ocher (powdered iron ore), weapons, tools, and the bodies of their dogs (Hudson 1976). To accompany the body to the next world, ornaments and other intimate possessions were placed with the body (Lewis and Kneberg, 1958).

Sometimes a stone pot was inverted over the head before the grave was filled; this was most often used for infants and younger children (Wimberly, 1980). Very young infants were apparently bound to their cradle boards in an extended or partly flexed position (Hudson, 1976). The graves were small circular pits dug into the shell mounds. The graves must have been marked in some manner since they were seldom disturbed by any later digging. These circular pits were usually sealed with a mud putty mixture consisting of clay, ash, and shell.

The Archaic Indians found it necessary to develop new weapons, tools, and utensils as well as ornaments. The early hunters' next great improvement in weaponry was the atlatl [at-lat-l], which allowed the hunter of the archaic period to throw with great force and to keep at a safe distance from animals (Brown and Owens, 1984). The atlatl was a piece of wood two or three feet long with a small base carved at the end. A weight was placed on the weapon to give added power. The hunter held the spear resting on the atlatl and against the notched end; then he lifted the atlatl over his shoulder and with a whip like motion, sent the spear hurtling toward the target (Brown and Owens, 1984). An atlatl hook made from antler and dating back to 4500 B.C. was found in the Stanfield-Worley Bluff Shelter which marks its earliest known use in North Alabama (Krebs, 1986). In addition, three atlatl ends were found in shell mounds in the mouth of Town Creek during the 1924 Smithsonian excavations.

The Archaic Indians made new points with side notches that made them easy to haft-tie to the shaft (Wimberly, 1980). Cutting tools and weapons used by Archaic Indians were chipped from flint or similar stone. One method used in making tools and weapons was pecking and grinding with stones that did not fracture easily. This process was used to make bowls of sandstone or soapstone. Hammer stones were made by pecking. In addition, grooved axes were manufactured and used into historic times (Vogel, 1982).

The primary method of making tools and weapons was pressure flaking and percussion. In percussion flaking, the flint is battered into shape with skillful blows from a hammer stone. In pressure flaking, a pointed tool of antler or bone is pressed against the edge to remove small flakes (Lewis and Kneberg, 1958). Greater precision in shaping and sharpening tools is possible by the pressure flaking technique. The Archaic Indians employed primarily the flaking method, but the grinding method was a part of their technology, although applied to only a few items (Lewis and Kneberg).

Flint tools were principally used to work antler, bone, and hides. Flint drills were used to bore holes in wood and other materials. Flint scrapes refined the finish on wooden, bone, and antler objects. Flint scrapers removed the flesh and hair from leather. Flint was used to make a variety of weapon points. Archaic Indians shaped their points in a basic triangular or oval blade shape. A variety of shapes were created by making notches at the base; or on the side near the base, or by removing both basal corners.

Fish nets, spears, traps, and hook and line were used to catch fish. Fish hooks were made from deer toe bones; sawed in half lengthwise; the central portion removed; then shaped into a strong hook. Traps were made by weaving reeds or oak splints into a conical shape where fish could swim in but not out. Evidence of fish traps are found all along Town Creek of Lawrence County. Remnants of stone dams are located at the downstream end of pool sections of the creek. Fish probably made up a major portion of the diet. Nets were made from fibers woven into loose netting, then attached to a hoop and weighted with shell sinkers. Indians used green cane spears with sharpened points (Hudson, 1976).

Archaic Indians in the Southeast began making pottery between one and two thousand years B.C. For the first time, early man had lightweight waterproof containers in which to store food and water. With pottery, he was able to stabilize his food supply and settle in more permanent surroundings. Some pottery found along the Tennessee River was in the form of open bowls. The pots had thick walls decorated with incised lines and punched indentations made by pressing a small tool into the wet clay before firing. The pottery was fiber tempered pottery, which means that fibers from grass, roots, and other materials were placed in the clay and the clay was strengthened by firing. Some pottery was more elaborately decorated with incised chevrons, diamonds, or squares on the outside of the bowls. Many various and different designs have been identified on pottery shards found along the Tennessee River of North Alabama.

There is little information on clothing and ornaments. Hides were processed and fashioned into clothing and footwear. Women were responsible for making the clothes from hides. Women were probably engaged almost continuously, in the processing of hides. The common method of preparing hides was to stretch the skin on the ground and scrap it, clean and tan it. The flesh was removed with a stone, bone, or antler scraper. Tanning was merely a matter of smearing the hide with fat, brains, and liver. The hides were then soaked in water. The skin was sometimes smoked. The hide was then stretched on a framework to dry. The leather was finally made pliable by working between the hands or sliding back and forth across a pole (Lewis and Kneberg, 1958).

Flint and bone tools were used in the leather working. Flint knives were used for cutting the leather. Sharp pointed pieces of bone called awls were used by Archaic Indians for sewing leather into clothes. The basic form of the needle, even to the elongated eye, invented in Paleolithic times in the Old World, has not changed today, except with respect to the material from which it is made (Hudson, 1958).

Archaic Indians adorned themselves with ornaments. Necklaces were made from animal or human teeth, beads of stone, shell, and rarely a copper bead or two. Copper beads and objects are common in Indian sites along the Tennessee River and throughout north Alabama. Bone bracelets were made from animal rib bones, bird bones, and bear teeth. Burial necklaces were often made from the vertebrae of a large rattlesnake strung together in place (Hudson, 1976). Among other odd items strung for necklaces were bear and bobcat eye teeth and turtle thigh bones (Hudson, 1958). Bone ornaments were often decorated with engraving. A need for material not found locally led to increased trade as well as social and religious interaction.

Archaic Indians had distinct characteristics. Archaic Indians seldom lived to be middle-aged; most died in their twenties and thirties. Archaic Indian skeletons show evidence that they suffered from arthritis. Root abscesses in their teeth were common and due to excessive wear from gritty food. In appearance they were at least two distinct types of Indians. One was broad-headed, broad-faced, squared-jawed, and had a narrow face and was generally less rugged in bone structure. The women were smaller and had a more jutting jaw than the men.

Archaic Indians were probably the first to domesticate dogs. The skeletons of rather large dogs, possibly hunting dogs, have been discovered in burial sites. Archaic Indians were the first to practice dog burials.

Archaic people were very abundant throughout the Lawrence County area based on numerous sites containing many archaic artifacts. The Oakville area along Flint Creek was a major archaic region. Many such archaic sites are found within the Moulton Valley of Lawrence County. Based on the size of archaic shell middens in the mouth of Town Creek; a significant number of archaic people inhabited the area of the Big Mussel Shoals for several hundred years. It is obvious that the archaic people of Town Creek would migrate to the shoals during low water periods to feast upon the fresh water mussels which could be gathered from the shallow water.

The Woodland Lifestyle of
The Warrior Mountains

This tradition gradually developed out of antecedents in the archaic tradition. In this new tradition, the Indians developed more and more refinements in ways of doing things and they learned to exploit particular foods of their local regions more efficiently (Brown and Owens, 1984). The Woodland people lived in small settlements which were more permanent than those of the archaic period.

A staple food supply encouraged the growth of people living in towns and hamlets. Improvement in pottery led to cooking by boiling. The saving and storing of seeds to ensure the next year's harvest encouraged the growth of more permanent groups of people. Hamlets consisted of a few farming families who shared hunting and gathering grounds. Towns possessed a market, a site for religious observances, and a nucleus for administrative officials (Vogel, 1982). One such Woodland Town was centered on the large ceremonial mound at Oakville in Lawrence County, Alabama.

The Copena Burial Mound at Oakville

Adequate food supplies allowed for the development of a more formalized leadership structure. These local and regional leaders guided religion and settled disputes. Leadership was an acquired status. In the beginning, status was not passed to children. As life became more complicated, the increasing importance and influence of these officials resulted in the development of hereditary ranks.

Early Woodland Indians were farmers, gatherers, and hunters. Early farmers grew gourds, squash, and primitive kinds of corn (Brown and Owens, 1984). Vegetable foods could be traded or easily stored; therefore, surplus became possible. Surplus food enabled some members of the community to devote their time to trade, crafts, politics, or religion. Hunting, fishing, and the collection of wild produce of the forest were still very important as the Indians used all that surrounded them (Brown and Owens, 1984). Floral remains from excavation sites reveal that the Woodland Indians ate hickory nuts, acorns, walnuts, and persimmons.

Tools used by the Woodland Indians were the bow and arrow, deer bones, stone hoes, grindstones, flaked tools. Dugout canoes were made of yellow pine or yellow poplar. Historic evidence suggests that wooden mortar and pestles were used to grind corn (Swanton, 1987). In the shift to the Woodland stage there was a change in the stone projectile point styles; while stemmed points continued to be made, triangular, un-stemmed varieties increased in frequency (Chapman, 1985).

The Hopewellian culture seems to have been centered in the states of Ohio, Illinois, Indiana, and Kentucky. Hopewellian ceremonial practices were present in cultures from the Great Lakes to Florida. This culture began at Poverty Point in Louisiana and progressed north and east. The Hopewells clothed themselves in fine furs, robes, well-tanned skins, and woven cloth. They decorated themselves with ornaments of copper, mica, shell and bone. Men and women alike wore ear decorations and necklaces of animal's teeth and pearls. The Hopewells were among North America's great prehistoric craftsmen and artists. The Hopewells made decorated pottery, finely woven mats, and exquisitely carved bone, wood, and metal figures. They were also fine metal workers crafting tools and ornaments from copper and occasionally silver and gold (Reader's Digest, 1978).

Burial customs were important to Woodland Indians. The noteworthy aspect of the Woodland Tradition was the construction of large burial mounds. These were conical mounds heaped with earth over burials. These mounds were sites of multiple burials. People were often buried with their personal possessions. A warrior was buried with weapons. A farmer was buried with agricultural tools. A woman was buried with household items. One single grave yielded 12,000 pearls, 35,000 pearl beads, 20,000 shell beads and nuggets of copper, iron and silver. Another grave yielded hundreds of pipes; copper figures of birds, turtles, and humans; a mask made from fragments of human skull; and a copper-covered wooden death effigy of the death cup mushroom.

In northern Alabama, the Copena buried copper and lead objects with their dead. The grooved, polished stone axes were replaced with un-grooved ones. Included in burial mounds was superior pottery made of clay mixed with sand, crushed pottery, and crushed stone. Human skulls were one of that people's most treasured cult symbols.

It is the Woodland Copena people that made Oakville their home. They constructed at least five mounds on the Oakville site. It appears from archaeological evidence that the Copena culture was extensive in Warrior Mountains of Alabama. The area of Oakville Indian Mounds Park is considered to have been the social and religious center of the Copena society of the Warrior Mountains.

The Alexander Mound, some three miles from Oakville, was excavated in 1924. It was a Woodland burial mound containing over 100 burials, Also found among the burials were conch shell cups, marble pipes, copper ear ornaments, celts of all sizes, and many other Woodland artifacts.

Mississippian Lifestyle of Warrior Mountains

The Mississippian tradition began spreading from the middle course of the Mississippi River to almost all parts of the Southeast. At the apex of its development, this tradition was the highest cultural achievement in North America. The population increased and towns grew up that were larger, more permanent, and more secularized than the large religious centers of the Woodland tradition (Brown an Owens, 1984). The Mississippian culture is marked by the appearance of distinctive forms of pottery which contained crushed shells in clay.

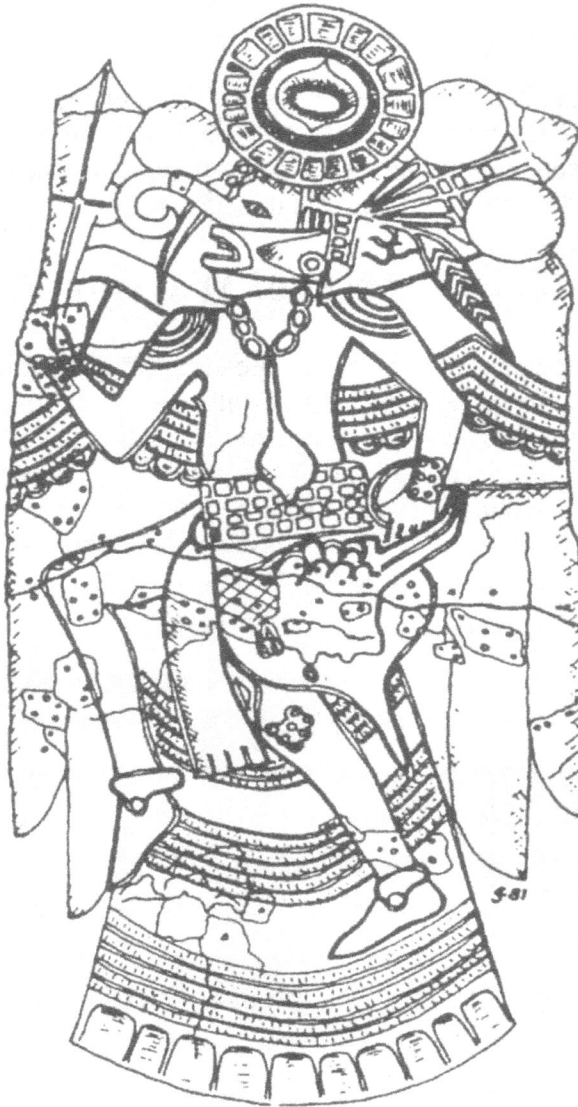

Temples, houses of the elite and council buildings were constructed around a central plaza of large earthen pyramids. Houses became more permanent. Cut saplings were placed in foundation trenches and pulled over at the top to form a roof superstructure. The walls were woven with cut branches, covered with clay, and the roof was covered with grass or bark.

Above: An artist's reconstruction of a Mississippian era temple mound at Florence, Alabama.
Below: Petroglyphs on a rock in the Kinlock Rockshelter.

The houses contained a hearth and sleeping benches. The houses measured about 16' x 16' feet. They had a centrally located fireplace to provide warmth in winter and protection from insects in the summer. They contained only a single room but used cane mats to divide the chamber. Cooking was done outside or in a cooking shed.

Religious ceremonialism was connected with agricultural production and centered on a fire-sun deity. The Mississippian people were involved in long distance trade. Territoriality and warfare increased during the Mississippian period. Highly organized chiefdoms emerged within the Mississippian culture.

Archaeological evidence indicates that the communities were divided into areas of public compound, domestic occupation, and area for industrial activities. Public buildings were located at the north end of the plaza. Industrial activities included pottery making, shell bead manufacturing, and the weaving of cane mats and baskets, the making of bone pins, fish hooks, and bone needles.

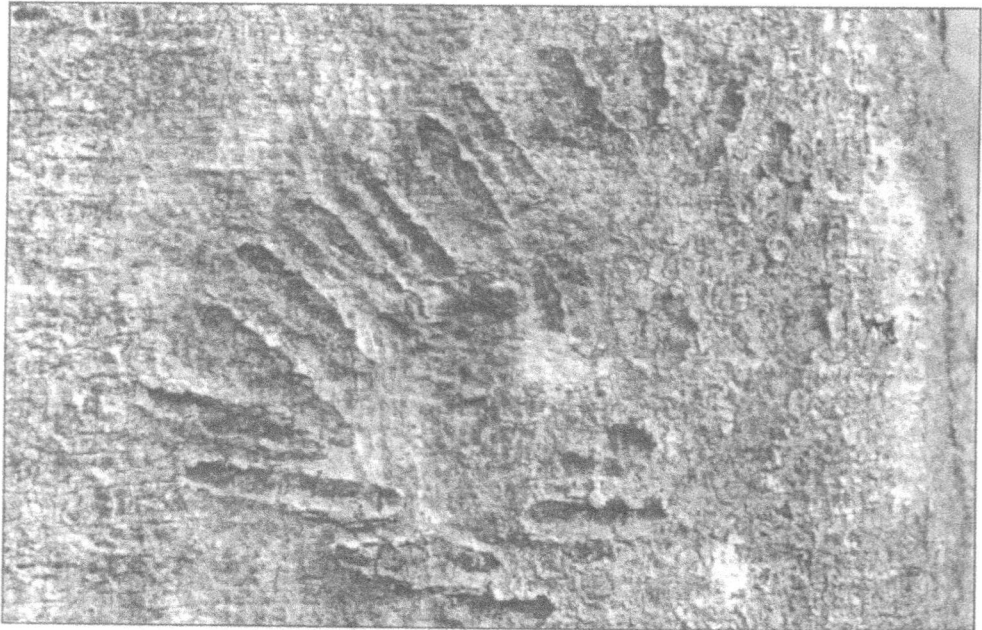

Indian arboglyph carved on a beech in the Bankhead Forest

Fortified settlements appeared during the Mississippian period. Wooden stockades with bastions constructed of closely set vertical posts were used. Dry moats with bastions constructed of closely set vertical posts were built around the stockades. Earthen embankments were also used as protective measure. Gunter's Landing near present day Guntersville was fortified with palisades. The Indian Mound village in Florence, Alabama was surrounded by an earthen embankment. Mounds were built around the plaza; some were for temples and some for burials. Temples contained images of animals or birds on the entrance. Temples were usually divided into two rooms - the first was used for worship; the second for funeral purposes. The southern Indians believed that the universe in which they lived was made up of three separate but related worlds: the Upper World, the Lower World, and This World.

According to the Cherokee doctrine, east was associated with the color red because it was the direction of the rising sun. East was also associated with the sacred fire, blood, and the color of success. West was the moon segment and because it was associated with the color black, which was the region of the souls and of death itself. North was the direction of the cold winds of the winter and its color was blue (sometimes purple) and it represented trouble and defeat. South was the direction of the warm winter sun, its color was white, and it was associated with peace and happiness.

Religious ceremonies were very important to the Mississippian Indians. Ceremonies related to death and burial became more important during the Mississippian period. In early times, family members were buried in a shallow hole in the floor the house; with each burial, the floor rose higher. During the Mississippian period, the Indians began building higher burial mounds. In one kind of mound, earth was piled on top of the place where the person was buried. Later, another body was buried and a pile of dirt was added on top. This was repeated until a large mound has been built. The new style of mounds served as the foundation for the temples or chiefs' house or other important buildings. Some mounds were 70 or 80 feet high with bases covering several acres (Examples: Oakville, Moundville, and Florence).

Forty mounds stand on 305 acres of flat land beside the Warrior River at Moundville, Alabama. A stairway of logs has been reconstructed on one side of the temple mound leading to the top. The original temple was probably built of mud-covered poles that had been pounded into the earth. A fire was kept constantly burning in the temple. The people worshipped a fire-sun god who brought good crop harvests.

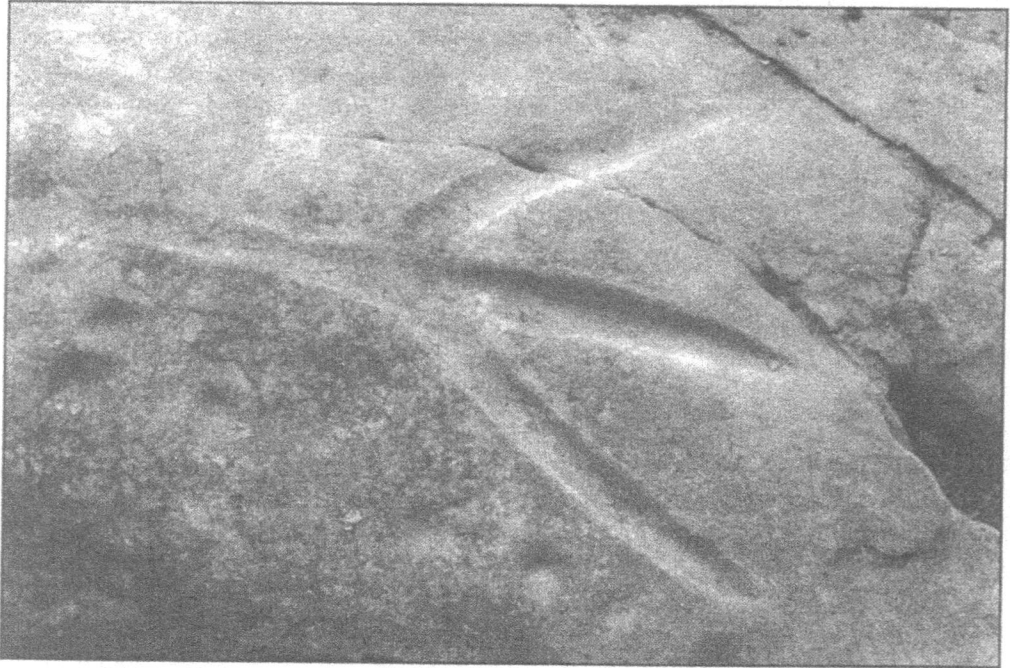

Mississippian era petroglyph in a bluff shelter, Warrior Mountains.

Ceremonial pipes were among the most sacred possessions of a tribe (Brown and Owens, 1984). The bowl of the pipe was carved from stone and decorated with animals or humans figures. The pipe stem was adorned with feathers or other materials. The Ceremonial pipe was passed around the council and each member took a puff before handing the pipe to the person on the left. The pipe came to be referred to as a peace pipe because they often smoked with former enemies as a peace treaty was made (Reader Digest, 1978).

Another belief relating to the spirit world concerns the black drink. It was brewed like a tea from the leaves of the holly plant (Ilex vomitoria). Black drink contained large amounts of caffeine and when heated and drank in large quantities caused vomiting. They believed that by emptying their stomachs they rid themselves of evil. They became purified in both body and soul and were ready to take part in religious ceremonies.

The Indians considered the land sacred; it could not be bought or sold. This idea was difficult for the white man to understand. Tecumseh, a Shawnee Chief, once said he could no more sell land than sell air or sea. Chickamauga Chief Doublehead of Lawrence County, Alabama was assassinated by his own people because he gave up Cherokee lands with the Cotton Gin Treaty of 1806.

The Southern Indians recognized a supreme being. The Creeks called him "Breath Maker" or "Master of Breath." The Cherokee called him "Yowa" (Brown and Owens, 1984). The Indians believed that tobacco was a sacred plant. They believed it was a gift from the spirit world with mystical powers. They smoked to ward of evil spirits. They smoked to curb appetites and cure infection. They smoked before they waged war. Smoking was done to ensure long-lasting affection between husband and wife.

A ritual called "remarking" was employed to call forth evil spirits, thus bring harm to one's enemies. The medicine man would hold the leaves up to the rising sun and murmur the appropriate incantation. He would knead the leaves into a wad by rolling the leaves in a counter clock direction. Sometimes he would spit in the sticky mess. Remarking was also used to conjure up the force of good. The medicine man took the leaves to the edge of a stream at dusk or midnight and rolled the wad of tobacco clockwise. A Cherokee who wished to rekindle or ensure his wife's love approached her when she was asleep and rubbed a mixture of tobacco and saliva over her body while he spoke the necessary incantation. A mixture of water and tobacco was rubbed on a patient's body who suffered from dog disease (stomach cramps).

The most important ceremony for the Creeks and other Southern tribes was the green com ceremony. The festival was like our Thanksgiving and New Year rolled into one. It was a time to give thanks for a successful harvest, to settle differences, and to begin a new year. The ceremony took place in July or August depending in when the corn was ripened.

The chief of each head town sent runners to smaller villages to tell the people when to come to the festival. The runners left a bundle of sticks in each village with instruction to break one stick each day; when all sticks were broken; it was time for the celebration. The first three days were spent cleaning the houses, public buildings, and themselves (ceremonial clean). On the third day, the most sacred part, the fire ritual, began. All the fires in the town were put out, even scared fires (Brown and Owens, 1984).

The starting of a new sacred fire was a religious rite, carried out by the high priest. For the occasion, the priest wore white buckskin clothes and white moccasins. To start the fire, he used a fire drill; twirling it in the sand and praying to the Breath Maker. Four logs in the form of a cross were pushed toward the fire. The priest took four ears of com and placed them in toward the fire. In this act, the priest made an offering to thanksgiving to the Breath Maker for another year. The fire of all the households was started anew from this scared fire.

The next five days of the festival were spent playing games and dancing. The women prepared food for the feast in the public square. Friendly rivalry between towns and clans was played on the ball field. The women danced, the men danced, and together they performed tribal dance. On the last day of the festival, a respected speaker of the tribe told the people to keep the ancient rites; he reminded them that they were bound together because they shared the same sacred fire.

Mississippian Era petroglyphs in Marion County, Alabama.

Games were an important part of the culture of the Southeastern Indians (Brown and Owens, 1984). The Southeastern Indians favorite game was called stickball or ball play also called lacrosse. It was so important that it was often called simply "the ball game." Stickball was played as part of the green corn ceremony. The game could be so rough that players broke arms, legs, or occasionally were killed. Each team had 60 or more players. Each player used 2 sticks or rackets. The rackets were 27 inches long. The rackets had a cup-like hoop at one end in which the hard deerskin ball could be caught.

The players could not touch the ball with their hands. The team lined up facing each other, the medicine man threw the ball high into the center of the field, and the struggle began to get the ball between the goals for a score. The only restriction was that the racket could not be used on another player. Much betting accompanied the game.

Chunkey was another favorite game of the Southern Muskhogean Indians. Two persons played at one time. One player started the game by rolling a smooth stone disk down the court. The object of the game was not to hit the stone but to throw the pole close to the spot where the disk stopped. The player whose pole landed nearest the disk made one point. If his pole actually touched the disk, the player made two points. Both players and spectators bet heavily on the outcome of the game.

Vegetables, wild fruits and nuts, wild animals and fish were main source of food. Indians spent much of their time farming. They grew corn, beans, squash, melons, pumpkins, and sweet potatoes. Indians made mush, dumplings, hominy, and succotash from corn. They gathered nuts, fruits, seeds, and roots from the woods and stored them. Hunting took second place to farming. The men showed skill in stalking and killing game. They killed turkey, raccoons, rabbits, pigeons, beavers, squirrels, and opossums. Fishing was done with spears and arrows, but most often by dragging seines made of brush fastened together with vines.

Clothing of Mississippian was very decorative. Among the Southeastern Indians, young children ran unclothed until their tenth or twelfth year. Girls were given a two-piece apron of mulberry tassels intertwined in a net foundation as their first garment. Later, they began to wear the knee length skirts of adult women. Older boys and men wore buckskin breechcloths. During warm seasons, both men and women, especially those of high status, donned deerskin or woven mantles dyed white or black and at times ornately painted. In winter months, men added a deerskin shirt and leggings tucked into the high, laced moccasins worn by all. Brightly colored bird feathers were used to decorate capes and were worn as hair ornaments.

Art forms of Mississippians were more advanced than that of the previous culture. Associated with the Southern Ceremonial Complex were a series of art forms on several media. These items were widely traded among distant settlements and ultimately ended up as mortuary offering in the graves of the civil, religious, and war leaders. This religious symbolism was engraved, painted, and sculptured on ceramics, copper, and dyed cloth. The major Southeastern Ceremonial Complex design elements found at Moundville can be divided into motifs, and representation of animals and humans (Walthall, 1977).

The Mississippian people of the Warrior Mountains appeared to be less densely populated than either the Woodland and Archaic inhabitants. Numbers of Mississippian artifacts do not compare in numbers as does the Archaic and Woodland; however, the length of time of habitation for Mississippian is less than that of Archaic and Woodland.

The First Indians of the Warrior Mountains

According to Vogel (1982), Alabama has more stone tools used by Paleo man than all of the western part of the United States. Many of these early stone tools could have been chipped and flaked from flint which occurs in the Tennessee Valley at the Elk River Shoals and Big Muscle Shoals on the Tennessee River. Besides providing Warrior Mountains' prehistoric Indians stone for tools, the Tennessee River was used as a major transportation route through North Alabama. From the river, early man could obtain a great variety of aquatic plants and animals that were an inexhaustible source of food. Along the bank of the river, early inhabitants could also find soil compatible to farming, and protective caves and bluff shelters to make camp.

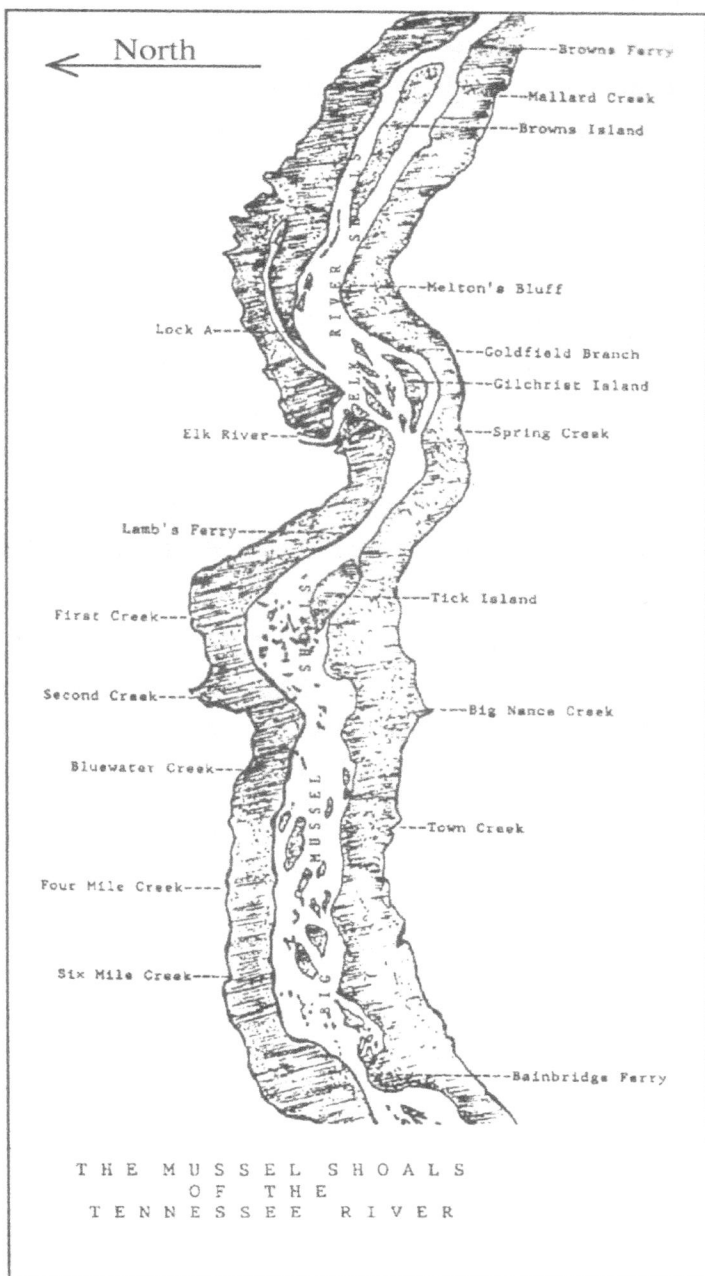

North

Browns Ferry
Mallard Creek
Browns Island

Melton's Bluff

Lock A
Goldfield Branch
Gilchrist Island

Elk River
Spring Creek

Lamb's Ferry

Tick Island

First Creek

Second Creek
Big Nance Creek

Bluewater Creek

Town Creek

Four Mile Creek

Six Mile Creek

Bainbridge Ferry

THE MUSSEL SHOALS
OF THE
TENNESSEE RIVER

24

The freshwater mussels found in the shoals were an important food supply for the tribes that settled in this region. The mussel shoals extended from present-day Lawrence County though Colbert County and had a fall of 134 feet within a distance of thirty-seven miles creating a vast series of rapids. According to Ortmann (1924), the mussel shoals received its name from the immense number if species and individuals of fresh-water mussels which used to be found at this locality. However, the present name "Muscle Shoals" appeared in the 1806 Treaty with the Cherokee Nation and has been repeated in official documents. While in 1892, the United States Geographic Board decided that in view of former official usage, the name should remain Muscle Shoals, yet much interest to archaeologist attaches to the term "mussel shoals" (Webb, 1939).

The Tennessee River has played an important role in the habitation of North Alabama, for in the Warrior Mountains of the north Alabama area originates the largest shoals in the Tennessee River. These shoals consist of Elk River Shoals, the Big Muscle Shoals, Little Muscle Shoals, Colbert Shoals, Bee Tree Shoals, and Waterloo Shoals.

The Elk River Shoals includes that portion of Tennessee River located in Lawrence County between what is known as Mallard Creek and Spring Creek. The Big Mussel Shoals started in Lawrence County in the area that is now Joe Wheeler State Park just a few miles west of Spring Creek and Elk River and some five miles east of Wheeler Dam. The Big Mussel Shoals extended into Colbert County. Little Mussel Shoals, Colbert Shoals, Bee Tree Shoals are located in the northwestern portion of the Warrior Mountains with the present day Wilson Dam located on the Little Muscle Shoals.

The mussel shoals had an abundance of aquatic life with the fresh water mussels being very numerous. The Indians depended upon these mussels as a seasonal source of meat for their diet. This bountiful supply of mussels caused many Indian tribes to settle in this area along the banks of the Tennessee River. Large shell mounds or middens (refuse deposits of mussel shells and garbage) have been found along the banks of the Tennessee River.

These mounds indicate that Indians groups lived here for long periods of time. Some of these shell mounds are forty feet in height and are composed mainly of mussel shells, though occasionally mounds of periwinkle shells are found (Soday, 1956).

Tremendous amounts of chert (flint) formed the erosion resistant layers of rock responsible for the shoals. The chert or flint rock is found for a mile or more along the Tennessee River in what is now Lawrence County at a place called Lock A. Flint rock was highly prized by the local prehistoric inhabitants for projectile points and tools. At least twenty-six sites of prehistoric Indian villages have been found in the Tennessee Valley along the river.

Although this area was occupied by other Indians, there were three identifiable groups who lived along the Tennessee River. The shell-mound archaic Indians were among the earliest Indians in the Tennessee Valley. The early woodland was of the specific archaeological complex of the Lauderdale Culture in North Alabama.

The Kinlock Rock Shelter contains rock carvings.

The Copena Indians of the Hopewell or middle woodland culture were the first Indians to use copper and galena extensively. Copena is a name derived from the combination of copper and galena. These were noted for mud putty burials containing copper and galena objects. The mud putty was mixture of clay, ash, and shell and was used to seal the burial. The burial mound at Oakville Indian Mounds Park was made by the Copena people as was the Alexander Mound that was excavated in 1924.

Many early Warrior Mountains Indians were shell-midden people and bluff dwellers. Evidence suggests that shell middens and bluff shelters were seasonal places of habitation. Shell middens were primarily used during the summer months when low water levels made the gathering of mussels easy. Most middens have alternating layers of sediment and mussel shells. High water levels would prevent gathering of mussels and also add layers of sediment to the midden.

Bluff shelters usually facing a southern direction were used during winter for protection from the elements. Numerous bluff shelters are located in Bankhead National Forest where the gathering of nuts, fruit, and other food was practicable. Two notable examples of bluff shelters in the Bankhead National Forest are the Kinlock shelters and McDougal sites. Probably in excess of 100 bluff shelters throughout the mountainous area were utilized as places of habitation by prehistoric Indian people. Petroglyphs (rock drawings) are found on the Kinlock Shelter, Courtland Mountain, and nearby Trapp Shelter in Franklin County.

Archaeological Sites of the Warrior Mountains

According to Webb (1939), a total of 237 Indians sites were identified in an archaeological survey of Wheeler Basin. The archaeological studies which are representative of prehistoric Indians people of North Alabama give insight into the times and lifestyle of Indians that once lived in and around the Warrior Mountains.

In Lawrence County, a total of thirty sites were listed which revealed there had been ten villages, thirteen mounds, four bluff shelters, two workshops and a cave (Gentry, 1962). These probably were those identified in the Wheeler Basin studies of the 1930's and did not include those south to the Warrior Mountains; therefore, this is not the total number of Indian village sites, bluff shelters, and caves in Lawrence County that have evidence of prehistoric and historic habitation. Much of the archaeological information in the area of the Warrior Mountains is lost forever to natural and man-made causes.

Stanfield-Worley Shelter

Stanfield-Worley Shelter is located in north central Colbert County seven miles south of the Tennessee River (Krebs, 1986). The bluff shelter or rock overhang was formed by soft Tuscumbia limestone eroded underneath forming a large protected cavity forty by two-hundred feet. Excavation has determined that four zones of stratum existed. The uppermost zone of stratum was loose gray brown soil which was two to four and one half feet deep. The first layer contained remains of ceramics produced during occupation of the shelter.

Prehistoric Indians lived in this shelter dating from 1500 B.C. to A.D. 1300. Burial pits found in this zone intruded into lower levels. Found at the bottom of the burial pit was an atlatl hook; this marked the atlatl's earliest known use in North Alabama. The second zone of stratum was of mottled soil about six inches thick that was capped by a fire-hardened clay floor. The third zone which was composed of yellow sand and clay ranged from four to six inches in thickness and did not contain any archaeological material.

The fourth and most significant layer of stratum, labeled zone D, was composed of brownish soil from two to six inches thick. This layer contained abundant artifacts and specimens dating from 7000- 7500 B.C. These artifacts included projectile points, uniface scrapers, gravers, and drills (Krebs, 1986).

Perry Site

The Perry Site is located twenty miles downstream from Wheeler Dam. The site is located at the upstream end of Seven Mile Island in the Tennessee River near Florence, Alabama (Krebs, 1986). The site is a large shell mound covering three hundred feet by two hundred feet and rises as much' as ten feet above the level of the island. The mound consists of layers of river carried sediments alternating with layers of mussel shells. Excavation concluded that the site was occupied by Shell Mound Archaic people during the warm season of the year.

The economic base for these people was hunting, fishing, collecting shellfish, and gathering wild plant foods. Large groups of people (perhaps one-hundred or more) occupied these shell mounds. During the cold seasons, the family group dispersed into upland areas. The lifestyle of these people was relatively simple-no permanent homes or villages and the political organization was of simple tribal level having no hereditary chief or leader. The artifacts found at this site included projectile points, knives and scrapers, fish bones, and a large necklace of marine shell beads which indicated trade with coastal people from the Gulf Coast (Krebs, 1986).

Hobbs Island

Hobbs Island is an excavation site located in the Tennessee River just south of Huntsville. The dates of this excavation are between 1935 and 1938. The excavation concluded that two villages existed between 1200-1700 A.D. The first village had twenty-one rectangular structures of both single post and wall trench types with a clay-lined fire basin in the center.

The second village had thirteen structure patterns of both the rectangular and circular design. The largest rectangular building measured 28 feet by 39 feet. The floor was clay lined and was eighteen inches below original ground level, a semi-subterranean structure. Interior post formed partitions in these dwellings. Five burial mounds were found at this site. These mounds were in the shapes of circles, ovals, and a truncated pyramid ranging two to ten feet high. The burial mounds contained skeletal remains of ninety Indians, decorated pottery vessels, shell gorgets, and marine shell artifacts.

Alexander Mound

The Alexander Mound is some three miles up-stream on the West Fork of Flint Creek from the Oakville Indian Mounds Park in Lawrence County, Alabama. The following newspaper article printed in the Moulton Advertiser on

November 27, 1924; gives insight into the Alexander Mound excavation: *"Indian Mound on Alexander Farm is Unusual"*

"Gerard Fowke of the Smithsonian Institution last week (1924) completed the excavation of the Indian mound on the Jake Alexander farm southeast of Moulton and reports great success. Where Mr. Fowke expected to find 5 to 10 skeletons, as is usually the case in a mound of this size, he found evidences of 106 burials, from very young children to very old people, some buried in an extended position on their backs, some on the "right side and others in a sitting or doubled up position, while in one place a number of bones were thrown in a pile indicating that they had been moved, from some other place.

The graves were of various depths from level with the surface of the ground to several feet below the surface. An interesting find was the skeleton of a child about five feet below the top of the mound with old fashioned hand-made nails lying on the bones. When the skull was reached it was found to be that of a Negro boy seven or eight years old, which had evidently been buried in the mound a century or more ago with no thought of it being an Indian cemetery.

Many fragments of various styles of decorated pottery were found, indicating that these Indians were of the Cherokee tribe or directly connected with them. One nearly complete tomahawk was round which measured seventeen and one-half inches long, the largest ever reported from this region. Many smaller tomahawks, skinning knives and arrow heads were found.

Two very fine large pipes and twenty spades used for agricultural purposes were among the valuable finds, also many shell and some copper beads, a copper gorget (a protective piece of armor for the throat or neck), and several conch shells.

One of the things which may be considered significant in connection with the old legend that somewhere in the mountains south of Moulton are vast deposits of lead ore, was the finding in this mound of many pieces of galena (lead) ore which had been or ked into various shapes.

Mr. Fowke says there are evidences of still other skeletons around the margin of the mound which he did not consider of sufficient value to dig out and it would have taken much extra digging to get to them.

He also stated that he had never opened another mound that paid as well in number of skeletons and other objects secured.

There are a number of other mounds located in the eastern part of Lawrence County, but Mr. Fowke predicts that none of them are likely to contain anything like the amount of valuable relic which this mound contained."

Tick Island

The following information was obtained from a study conducted in the Wheeler Basin portion of our county prior to the impoundment of Wheeler Reservoir. Tick Island, presently flooded by Wheeler Lake, is approximately two miles upstream from Wheeler Dam near the south bank of the Tennessee River.

Both shell mounds and burial mounds were discovered on this now flooded island in the Tennessee River. A spot on Tick Island had refuse from Indian settlements that reached a depth of more than eight feet for an area of nearly two acres. Mounds of this type were often as much as 300 feet wide, 600 feet long, and fifteen to twenty feet high. They had as much as 60,000 cubic yards of materials, essentially all the leftovers from primitive kitchens (Gentry, 1972).

Shell mounds were composed of mussel shells, animal bones, stones, pebbles, flint chips, fashioned or broken objects, potsherds, fish remains, charcoal, and occasionally human burials. At a mound site on Tick Island, water bottles, utility vessels and pottery shards made by sand after it was constructed. The pottery was a mortuary offering buried with the dead that had extended or flexed and sometimes the bones were buried in bundles (Gentry, 1962).

Lamb's Ferry

Lamb's Ferry was an excavation site at a cave situated twenty feet up a bluff on the Tennessee River. The Lamb's Ferry cave is located in Lawrence

County about five miles upstream from Wheeler Dam approximately halfway between the Dam and Spring Creek. Skeletal remains at this site indicated average size of an individual to be medium height, rather light-boned, and broad-faced with high cheek bones (Gentry, 1962).

Hood Harris Mound

The Hood Harris Site was a mound located 100 yards east of Big Nance Creek, about four miles from the mouth of the creek. The conical burial mound which was nine feet high with a basal diameter of seventy feet was discovered at this site. Artifacts unearthed at this location were skeletal remains, two interlocked copper reel-shaped objects, strings of copper beads, large balls of worked galena, and stalactite effigy pipes (one pipe represented a dog).

Other Prehistoric Sites

Archaeological evidence in north Alabama spans over 10,000 years of time and covers our entire area from the north of the great Tennessee River to the southern end of the beautiful Warrior Mountains including the William B. Bankhead National Forest. Through thousands of years of habitation, the red man left an eternal mark upon our county with his stone tools. These implements of livelihood are still cherished by his aboriginal descendants and stand as a reminder of how deep our roots are planted in Tennessee Valley soil.

A burial mound and ceremonial mound are located at the present-day Oakville Indian Mounds Park in Lawrence County, Alabama. Within five miles of the Oakville site are many more Indian mounds sites which were associated with the religious, social, and cultural center at Oakville.

Other Indian mounds, some of which are not well defined, are scattered throughout Lawrence County. Most Indians mounds located in or near Lawrence County are eroded by farming or have been dug and looted by people who have no regard for scientific archaeological excavation.

Gilchrist Island is located near the mouth of Spring Creek and Brown's Island is located near the mouth of Mallard Creek in the Tennessee River. These islands, including the islands that formed the Elk River Shoals, are now flooded by Wheeler Lake. All the major islands in the Muscle Shoals were used by the prehistoric and historic Indians of the Tennessee Valley.

Numerous bluff shelters throughout the Warrior Mountains show signs of prehistoric habitation. Many caves are found throughout Lawrence County's limestone formations but no known survey of prehistoric habitation has been conducted.

Many Indian village sites exist along the Tennessee River and its tributaries which flow through the Warrior Mountains. Major tributaries in Lawrence County where surface collections of Indians artifacts occur include West Flint, Elam, Fox's, Mallard, Spring, Big Nance, and Town Creek. Most village sites in the Warrior Mountains occur near natural springs with an abundant water supply.

West Fork of Flint Creek in the Bankhead National Forest.

Bankhead Forest in Lawrence County has evidence of prehistoric occupation by Indians along its numerous streams and bluff lines. The Tennessee River also had numerous Cherokee towns including Monee Town or Mouse Town at the mouth of Fox's Creek (named after principal chief of the Cherokees Black

Fox); Fox's Stand at the junctions of the Black Warriors' Path and Brown's Ferry Road; Doublehead's Town at the Brown's Ferry crossing of the Tennessee River; Melton's Bluff eight miles west of Brown's Ferry; Cuttatoy's Village on Gilchrist Island at mouth of Spring Creek; Gourd's Settlement at present-day Courtland; and Shoal Town at the mouths of Town Creek, Big Nance, and Blue Water Creeks are historic Indian towns in Lawrence County, Alabama.

Early Historic Indians of the Warrior Mountains

Desoto's 1540 Invasion of North Alabama

Hernado DeSoto, a Spanish explorer, was the first European to move inland to the heart of Indian country. DeSoto had been with Cortez in Mexico when he conquered the Aztec and became a very rich man. He was also with Pizarro in South America when Pizarro robbed and killed many of the Incas. DeSoto's goal was to conquer the southeastern Indians, steal their gold, and become a very wealthy man.

On June 28, 1540, DeSoto crossed the Tennessee River and entered Alabama. He was the first European to discover the Tennessee River. DeSoto entered Alabama in Jackson County, and crossed the Sand Mountain. U.S. Highway 72 from Bridgeport toward Scottsboro in Jackson County follows near the route which DeSoto used on the first leg of his exploration. From June 1540 until December 1540, DeSoto traveled through Jackson, Marshall, Etowah, St. Clair, Calhoun, Talladega, Coosa, Elmore, Montgomery, Autauga, Lowndes, Dallas, Wilcox, Monroe, Clarke, Marengo, Hale, Greene, and Pickens Counties of Alabama. The Federal government appointed a commission of scholars to make a detailed study of DeSoto's route to clarify the contradictions that have arisen about exploration. Dr. Walter B. Jones was secretary of the commission. The Final Report of the DeSoto Commission was published in 1939.

DeSoto's party consisted of about 600 men and in addition numerous Indians who went along as guides, laborers, and bearers of burdens. In DeSoto's army, there were a number of Portuguese and a mixture of other nationalities, although most were Spaniards. DeSoto brought Negro slaves into Alabama which were probably the first Negroes to enter Alabama. With DeSoto came a few high born nobles and many plain men, including artisans of various trades: carpenters, shoemakers, tailors, blacksmiths, sword makers, soldiers, seamen, and priests. DeSoto obtained food by seizing it from the Indians who has stored up small amounts for their own use.

At Tali, DeSoto crossed the Tennessee River for the third time and entered the Indian village of Coosa. Coosa was the center of a prosperous Creek Indian agricultural complex. The Indian village of Coosa was located near the present-day Childersburg. Coosa was the upper of the two capitols of the Creek Indians. Today, one would pass through or near DeSoto Country while traveling to the following cities: Albertville, Atalla, Gadsden, Talladega, and Childersburg. It was DeSoto's custom to seize Indian chiefs who were then held hostage to ensure that DeSoto got what he wanted.

On August 20, 1540, DeSoto's men left the village of Coosa; and on August 31, they arrived at Ulibahali. Ulibahali was located on the north side of the Tallapoosa River. Ulibahali was about halfway between the big bend in the Tallapoosa and the point where it joins the Coosa River between Montgomery and Wetumpka. From Ulibahali, DeSoto and his men went to Talisi, the northwestern edge of present-day Montgomery where Maxwell Air Force Base now stands.

It was at Talisi that DeSoto encountered the son of Chief Tuscaloosa; therefore, he released the Coosa chief who was being held hostage. Leaving Talisi, the Spaniards proceeded through present-day Dallas County to Cax near the mouth of Cedar Creek. From here, DeSoto moved southward to Camden and through Wilcox County into Monroe County to the Indian village of Piache. The Spaniards moved from Piache to Mabila, one of the most important places to DeSoto's men and to Alabama History.

At Mabila on October18, 1540, was fought one of the bloodiest battles with any Indians on American soil. DeSoto was living on the spoils of the land since his supply base was in Cuba. The Indians were anxious to protect their winter food supply. The Spaniards were willing to fight the Indians because they had armor to protect themselves from Indian arrows. The greatest advantage of all advantages was the fact that the Spaniards had horses. It is very unlikely that even a determined man like DeSoto would have tried to crack the hard problem of the Alabama wilderness if the Spaniards had not so many advantages over the Indians.

DeSoto and giant Chief Tuscaloosa, **Black Warrior**, as portrayed in the History of Alabama, 1938.

In the Battle of Malbila, the Indians were led by a giant of a man Chief Tuscaloosa. Since Tuscaloosa means Black Warrior, the river bears his name. DeSoto tried to win Chief Tuscaloosa's friendship by giving him presents such as a scarlet suit, cap, and the largest horse he possessed. In spite of DeSoto's outward show of friendship, it soon became clear to Tuscaloosa that DeSoto intended to make him a prisoner.

When the Indians realized that Chief Tuscaloosa was a prisoner, they were ready to fight. It was a fierce battle that lasted all day. When it became clear that Spanish were winning, several Indians committed suicide. The Spaniards set fire to the Indian village. DeSoto was wounded and about twenty Spaniards and an estimated 2,500 Indians were killed.

Although wounded, DeSoto continued his journey toward the Gulf of Mexico to meet with Francisco Maldonado, who was bringing fresh plies. Because DeSoto had not succeeded in finding gold and could not accept defeat, he decided move northward away from Maldonado.

DeSoto remained at Mablia from October 18 to November 14, 1540, to allow his men to recover from battle. Although DeSoto never found the gold he so desperately sought in Alabama, DeSoto became one of the most famous explorers anywhere in the world.

DeSoto departed Mabila on November 14, 1540, and moved northward to the Black Warrior River. The country he traveled is today U.S. Highway 43 from Grove Hill to Thomasville, Dixons Mill, Linden, and Old Spring Hill. From Old Spring Hill, DeSoto passed a few miles east of Demopolis toward Greeneburg and crossed the Black Warrior River ere he found four Indian villages.

From these villages, DeSoto moved north and then west through present-day Eutaw in Green County and from there across the Sipsey River. They passed near Carrolton in Pickens County and moved across the present-day Alabama State line into Mississippi.

DeSoto was the first European to discover the Tennessee River, the Coosa, the Tallapoosa, the Alabama, the Black Warrior, the Sipsey River, the Tombigbee, and many lesser creeks and streams of Alabama (Summersell, 1981).

Diseases Transmitted by Europeans

New world diseases were among the greatest killers of Southeastern Indian people. Epidemics of lethal pathogens began to spread widely through the Native American population no later than A.D. 1520 and did not end until 1918 (Dobyns, 1983). The devastation of disease helped break the power of Native Americans and left them vulnerable to cultural change brought by invading Europeans.

When Europeans came to the New World, they brought several diseases for which the Indians had no immunity. The first meeting between Europeans and Southeastern Indians for which we have adequate documentation came in 1513 with Ponce de Leon on the Florida Coast. Indians contracted diseases from sailors whose European ships briefly touched the coast or from shipwrecked sailors. In 1521, a party led by a captain came ashore in the vicinity of Winyaw Bay, South Carolina where the Indians were invited to visit the ships and were promptly enslaved. Many of the enslaved Indian prisoners on the ship fell ill and died.

When DeSoto reached Cofitachequi in central South Carolina, he found whole villages wiped out because of the epidemic. Confitachequi was one of the most impressive Indian societies that DeSoto encountered. This town contained one of the most impressive examples of native architecture that DeSoto witnessed. The town itself was deserted because of depopulation caused by the plague.

The paleo ancestors of the Southeastern Indians left the diseases of the Old World behind; but when the Old World diseases reached New World shores, the Indians met with disaster. The most lethal pathogen Europeans introduced to Native Americans in terms of the total number of casualties was smallpox (Dobyns, 1983). Smallpox was the most terrible of the new diseases. Other diseases included measles, typhus, tuberculosis, chicken pox, and influenza. Europeans had been exposed to these diseases for many centuries and had acquired a resistance to them so they usually recovered.

Smallpox is extremely communicable, especially under crowded conditions. Among the previously unexposed New World population, smallpox would infect almost every individual and 30 percent or more of those infected would die. After an incubation period of about twelve days, the victim of smallpox suffers from high fever and vomiting, and three or four days later his body becomes covered with skin eruptions. For those who survive the disease, the eruptions dry up in about a week or ten days and the scabs fall off leaving disfiguring pockmarks. Some Indians were made blind by this disease. People who survive are immune for a period of time (Dobyns, 1983).

Measles, also caused by a virus, may have been the second largest killer of Native Americans. Spaniards transmitted this scourge of disease to Native Americans in 1531. Thousands of these natives died because they contracted measles when they were pressed into service. Between 1530 and 1900, there were at least 15 epidemics of measles. Influenza may have been the third most lethal disease of Native Americans. At least ten influenza epidemics or combinations of influenza with other diseases caused many deaths. A combination of influenza with smallpox or with another rash-producing virus caused extremely high mortality.

Bubonic plague vied with influenza as the third largest killer of Native Americans. The Black Death that had terrified Europe reached the New World in 1545 and was transmitted to man by fleas that lived on rats. There were four epidemics of the plague between 1545 and 1707. Diphtheria caused by a bacillus, became epidemic on at least five occasions during the 17th and 18th centuries caused tremendous numbers of deaths. Typhus, a deadly rickettsia disease, was difficult to diagnose prior to the mid-nineteenth century. Ship's typhus was common among crews and passengers on European sailing ships carrying people and goods to the New World. There were four documented epidemics and other probable ones between 1580- 1740.

During the 19th century, Native Americans suffered with immigrant Europeans from worldwide cholera epidemics in 1832-1834, 1849, and 1867. Cholera was transmitted by water infected by the disease germ. U.S. troops often transmitted the disease to Native Americans. Scarlet fever was not identified by the medical profession as a distinct affliction until the 18th century. Other diseases of lesser significance among Native Americans were whooping cough, malaria, and mumps. There are also indications that Native Americans suffered from diabetes (Readers Digest, 1978).

Trade between Southern Indians and Europeans

Trade between Europeans and Alabama Indians was based largely on the barter of animal skins (furs and hides). An Indian could swap about 30 deerskins for a new rifle. With rifle obtained through fur trade, the Indians in Lawrence County and North Alabama became more proficient in killing game. Native animals such as whitetail deer, black bear, eastern cougar, timber wolves, and eastern elk became depleted throughout the Southeastern United States. The commercialized fur trade with the Indians and afterward with early settlers led to the extirpation of these magnificent animals from Lawrence County and North Alabama by the early 1900's.

Iron trade Tomahawks

European trade with the Southern Indians opened a new era in American history. Southeastern Indian trade was mainly among the countries of Spain,

Britain, and France. Trade with the various European countries was separated geographically. Spain controlled trade in Florida and surrounding areas. France controlled trade in Louisiana and the Mississippi River area. Britain controlled trade in the Atlantic coast area.

The main items of trade were deerskins and Indian slaves. In the short term, the trade in deerskins and Indian slaves was a way in which the British could market some of their manufactured goods-guns, tomahawks, hoes, brass kettles, knives, rum, beads, hawk bells, and cloth. In the long term, it was their way of reducing them to dependent status and of disrupting and destroying them. The Indians found that they could not exist without cloths, tools, and ammunition. As the traders became economically necessary to the Indians, they found they could manipulate the Indian. The traders lived dangerous lives; more often than not the Indians hated them. Spurred by economic necessity the Indians very rapidly depleted the deer population.

From 1699 to 1715, Carolina exported an average of 54,000 deerskins per year. The greatest number of deerskins in anyone year was 121,355 in 1707. In addition to trading for skins, Southeastern traders continued doing business in Indian slaves. In 1708, the total population of South Carolina was 9,580 including 2,900 blacks, and 1,400 Indian slaves. In 1712, an Indian man or woman sold for 18 to 20 pounds. The French justified Indian slavery on the ground that it saved them from cruel deaths at the hands of their enemies.

The Yamasee War, caused over trade, was a widespread revolt against the Carolina traders by the Creeks, the Choctaws, some Cherokees and some of the Indians who lived along the Savannah River. Because of the war, the Indians found themselves in debt. In 1711, an estimated debt to the traders amounted to 100,000 deerskins; this meant that each male Indian was in debt for about two years of his labor.

The deerskin trade crumbled during the hostilities, and it was not fully rebuilt until 1722. After the war, the British power waned, and French and Spanish power was enhanced. The Lower Creeks allowed the French to build Fort Toulouse on the Alabama River in 1717. Unlicensed traders "the lowest people" used rum to get the Creeks and Cherokees drunk and then cheated them out of their deerskins (Swanton, 1987).

Early Population Estimates for Southern Tribes

Early population estimates based on census records for the four major tribes of Southeastern Indians are inaccurate, since the records did not declare the degree of Indian blood necessary for a person to be an Indian. Many mixed-blood Indian people avoided census records because the first Indian census was for enrollment for removal and for appraisal of their property. Therefore, the 1832 and 1835 Indian census records missed many mixed-blood people who were one-quarter or less Indian because it was very unpopular to be declared Indian. Even the President of the United States showed open dislike of all Indian peoples.

Cordeila Gray, Cherokee, Mother of Dollie Riddle

President Jackson on Indian Removal, December 8, 1829: *"A portion, however, of the Southern tribes, having mingled much with the whites and made some progress in the arts of civilized life, have lately attempted to erect en independent government within the limits of Georgia and Alabama. These States, claiming to be the only sovereigns within their territories, extended their laws over the Indians, which induced the latter to call upon the United States for protection. But it seems to me visionary to suppose that in this state of things claims can be allowed on tracts of country on which they have neither dwelt nor made improvement, merely because they have seen them from the mountain or passed them in the chase,"* (Prucha, 1975).

Mary Tennessee Garrison, ¾ Cherokee, wife of Will Spillers

Many mixed-blood people were not perceived as being Indian, since most were taught the ways of their European parent and did not live as full blood Indian people. After Indian removal in 1838, it would have been very foolish for a mixed-blood Indian person in Mississippi, Alabama, and Georgia to declare himself an Indian. The post removal period was a time for mixed-blood Indians to deny their race unless they were willing to give up all they had and be placed on reservations.

Brady Walker father of author, 7/16 Creek/Cherokee

The Cherokee population ranged from 22,000 in 1650 to 22,804 in the "1835 Census of the Cherokee Indians east of the Mississippi." The Choctaw population ranged from 15,000 in 1650 to 15,911 in the 1910 Census. The Chickasaw population ranged from 8,000 in 1650 to 10,956 in 1919 which included 5,659 by blood, 645 intermarried, and 4,652 in 1832-1833 Census; however, many tribes made up the Creek Confederation.

Historic Indians of the Warrior Mountains

1650 to 1817 Indians of the Warrior Mountains

The Creek Nation claimed and ruled over the mountainous forest area of Warrior Mountains from prehistoric time until 1814. The Cherokee, Yuchi, Shawnee, Creek, Chickasaw, and again the Cherokee respectively claimed territory in the Tennessee River portion of the Warrior Mountains from 1540 to 1816. Therefore, it seems the Tennessee Valley portion of north Alabama was in continuous dispute during historic times. Much Indian blood was probably shed over the waterways, the Great Mussel Shoals, and abundant wildlife found throughout the valley area.

Early traders recognized the wealth that lay within the Indian nations and rapidly became a part of those Indian people through intermarriage. Historic Indians known to have lived in Warrior Mountains were: Yuchi of the Uchean stock; Creek and Chickasaw of the Muskhogean stock; Cherokee from the Iroquoian stock; and Shawnee of the Algonquian stock.

According to the traditional history of the Cherokees, they were the. first inhabitants of the Tennessee Valley from which for some reason they retired about 1650, retaining a claim upon it, however, as their hunting ground (Leftwich, 1935). Then in 1770, the powerful Chickamauga Cherokee Chief Doublehead and his confederacy of Lower Cherokee, Yuchi, Chickasaw, Creek, Delaware, Shawnee, mixed blood Celtic people, and Scots-Irish connected by marriage established Doublehead's Town at the Brown's Ferry crossing in Lawrence County, Alabama near the head of Elk River Shoals.

The Yuchi of the Uchean stock were known to have lived here in the early 1700's (Swantons, 1987). A band of Yuchi seems to have lived at a very early date near Muscle Shoals on the Tennessee River, whence they probably moved into east Tennessee near the Hiwassee River and south near the Chattahoochee River. In 1714, a dispute between the Yuchi and Cherokee at Hiwassee caused the Yuchi to flee to Florida; but many of them certainly remained in the Cherokee country for a long time afterward, and probably eventually migrated west with their host (Swanton, 1952). Also, a band of Yuchi left the Shoals of the

Tennessee Valley and traveled south along Black Warriors' Path to a place now called Euchee Creek in Russell County, Alabama. It is thought these people intermarried with the Creek people.

Chickamauga Cherokee Chief Dragging Canoe

The Chickasaw, Creek, Cherokee, and Shawnee were also a part of the Chickamauga Confederacy and their territories overlapped in the Warrior Mountains. The Chickasaw and the Creek were of Muskhogean stock, and the Shawnee were of Algonquian stock.

Jim Sawgrass, modern Creek Indian

The Creek Indians controlled the mountainous area in the southern portion of Warrior Mountains from prehistoric times through the early 1800's. As a war indemnity, the Creek were forced to give up by the Treaty of Fort Jackson on August 9, 1814, most of their domain in Alabama, including the area that in now Cullman County (Jones, 1972). The Treaty of 1814 included Creek land claims in the southern portion of Lawrence County south of High Town Path. The first homestead claims in Winston County were made in 1814 near the present-day Town of Lynn; Richard McMahan settled near present-day Haleyville in 1815 (Thompson, 1968).

Rabbit Town in Bankhead Forest could very likely be the location of the Creek town mentioned by Swanton. It is obvious that Bankhead Forest was a staging area for Creeks fighting against the Chickasaw and eventually working with Chief Doublehead, a Chickamauga Cherokee. Many of the Creek Indians probably joined and lived with the Cherokees in Tennessee Valley of the Warrior Mountains.

The Shawnee were eventually forced out of the Tennessee Valley, and the Chickasaws won claims to the western Tennessee Valley area over the Creeks. In 1715 and again in 1745, the Chickasaws and the Cherokees joined to expel the Shawnees (Leftwich, 1835). During 1769, a Cherokee force challenged the Chickasaws at the original Chickasaw Old-fields located along the Tennessee River near Huntsville and were soundly defeated (Gibson, 1970). The Chickasaws, who had never know defeat but paid such a dear price for victory over the Cherokees, decided to abandon their settlement but not their claim to country (Leftwich, 1935).

The Cherokee of the Iroquoian stock were the last group of Indians to live in the Lawrence County area and moved here between 1770 and 1780. Oka Kapassa, a Cherokee village, was established about 1780 on the west bank of Coldwater or Spring Creek, at its confluence with Tennessee, just west of the present Tuscumbia (Harris, 1977). The name Oka Kapassa, a Choctaw-Chickasaw word meaning "Coldwater," would indicate that Chickasaws had a village on the site before the Cherokee planted one there (Leftwich, 1935).

The Creeks continued encroachment into Lawrence County after the Cherokees moved back into the area. The Creeks made their presence known in Lawrence County until the early 1800's. Prior to 1800, the Chickamauga Creeks and Cherokees lived and worked together within the Great Bend of the Tennessee River. During early migration by white settlers into Indian country, Cherokees and Creeks were living in the same villages in Lawrence and Colbert Counties. Conflicts occurring between the Cherokees and Creeks in Lawrence County forced some of the Cherokees to move to the north side of the Tennessee River (Royall, 1818). The conflicts occurred because of a demand from the United States in 1813-1814 that the Cherokees take up arms against the hostile Creeks (Woodward, 1963).

In a treaty on March 22, 1816, the Cherokee-Creek boundary was clarified by the Creeks recognizing Cherokee land claims south of the Tennessee River. The Treaty granted the United States free use of all roads and navigation of all rivers within Cherokee Territory. The Treaty also permitted the Cherokee to erect "stands" (taverns) and other public buildings along these roads (Woodward, 1963).

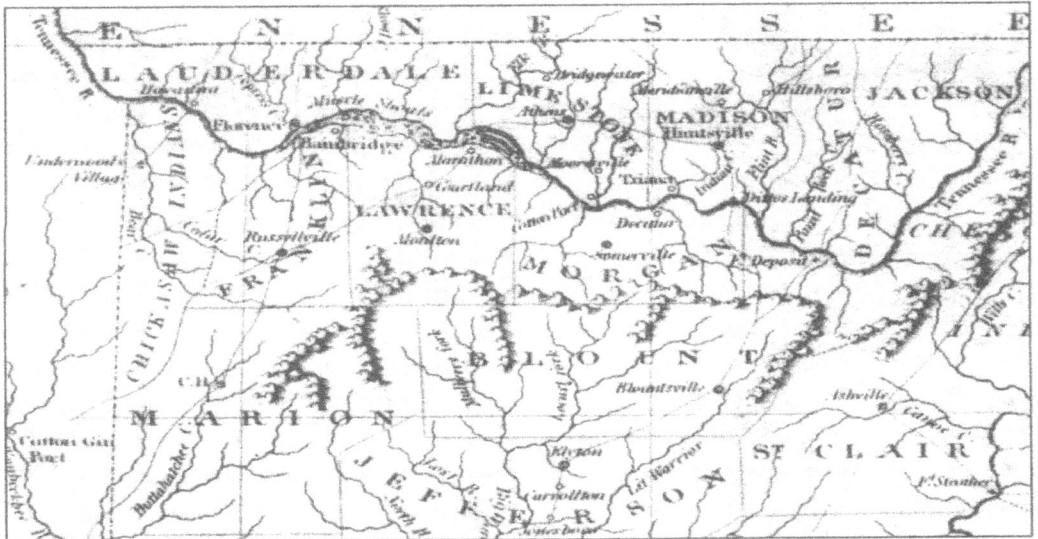

1825 Map of the Warrior Mountains

The large move of Cherokee Indians, the late comers to the Lawrence County area, into Alabama was under the leadership of Dragging Canoe, who was the son of Attakullaculla. On March 17, 1775, the Cherokee ceded to the Federal government a large of land at the site of Sycamore Shoals in upper Tennessee (Woodward, 1963). Two chiefs, Oconostota and Attakullaculla signed the treaty which was violently opposed by Dragging Canoe because the treaty gave away Cherokee lands. Nancy Ward was unsuccessful in the attempt to maintain peace. Dragging Canoe and his followers-Doublehead, Young Tassel, Bloody Fellow, and Ositto declared war against the settlers (Woodward, 1963); The war which was started on July 8, 1776. Doublehead, who led to the Cherokee settlement in Tennessee Valley portion of the Warrior Mountains, was a feared Chickamauga war leader of the western Chickamauga Confederacy.

As Dragging Canoe and his followers moved down the Tennessee River, they worked with the Creeks forced the Chickasaws westward. The Chickasaw eastern boundary became Caney Creek in what in now Colbert County; however, they never relinquished their claims to the land east to the Chickasaw Oldfields near Huntsville, Alabama. Dragging Canoe, who was at the height of his power 1788-1792, established the five lower Cherokee towns along the Tennessee River from Chattanooga, Tennessee to Scottsboro, Alabama. Shortly before the death of Dragging Canoe, Doublehead became a powerful warrior of the mussel shoals.

On September 1, 1788, Congress issued a proclamation forbidding white intrusion into Cherokee Territory. An unauthorized white settlement was established near mussel shoals by Franklinite settlers from the State of Franklin in present day Tennessee causing Dragging Canoe and his followers to besiege the settlement there. They burned its fortifications and drove the Franklin settlers out of area of the shoals. Dragging Canoe and his followers were referred to as Chickamaugans (Woodward, 1963).

In the Cotton Gin Treaty of 1806, lands north of Tennessee River were ceded by the Cherokee chiefs, Doublehead and Tahlonteskee, to the federal government. The Cotton Gin Treaty was consummated in December, 1806 with Doublehead and other Cherokees. At the time, Chief Doublehead was in Lauderdale County near Blue Water Creek; prior to the treaty, Doublehead lived at Doublehead's Town near Brown's Ferry in Lawrence County, Alabama. He had help establish villages all the way down the Tennessee River to the place where the Natchez Trace crossed the river in Colbert County. In 1790, Chief Doublehead founded the Natchez Trace village with the aid of forty Creek and Cherokee warriors (Harris, 1977). Doublehead, known as a cruel, bloodthirsty killer, raided the Cumberland settlements of Tennessee and firmly established the Chickamauga presence in the Tennessee Valley of north west Alabama.

During the Cotton Gin Treaty negotiations, Chief Doublehead leased 1,500 acres in Lauderdale County for 99 years, renewable 900 years (McDonald, 1977). Doublehead was executed on August 9, 1807 by the Cherokee because he had violated the sacred unwritten law which prohibited cession of Cherokee lands without the National Council's consent.

In the spring of 1808, Thomas Jefferson, then President of the United States, proposed to Tahlonteskee that he could escape punishment if he and his followers would agree to move west. Tahlonteskee, fearing assassination, accepted, and moved in the summer of 1809; this group became known as "Cherokees West" or "Old Settlers." Tahlonteskee and some 1131 Cherokees left Lawrence and Lauderdale Counties from Shoal Town (Town Creek-Bluewater village) on the Tennessee River to become the first Cherokees removed west from the western portion of the Tennessee Valley's Muscle Shoals.

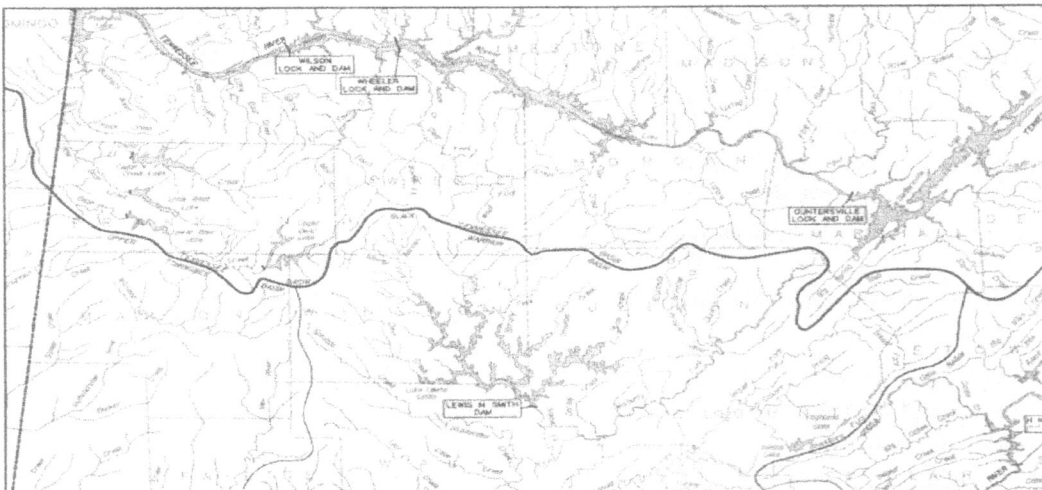

The Tennessee Divide separates the drainages of the Black Warrior and Tennessee Rivers and was used as the Indian boundary and trail known as the High Town Path.

Much of the area along the Tennessee River from Huntsville westward was claimed by both the Cherokee and Chickasaw Tribes. According to the terms of the Turkey Town Treaty, on September 14, 1816, the United States government paid the Cherokee $65,000.00 for their territory south of the Tennessee River and east to Marshall County (Jones, 1972). On September 18, 1816, the Chickasaws were paid $124,000.00 for their land east of Caney Creek in Colbert County, Alabama. On July 8, 1817, worn down by Andrew Jackson and perhaps by bribery, the Cherokees gave up land which later became Morgan, Lawrence, and Franklin Counties in return for the equivalent in land on Arkansas and White Rivers (Woodward, 1973).

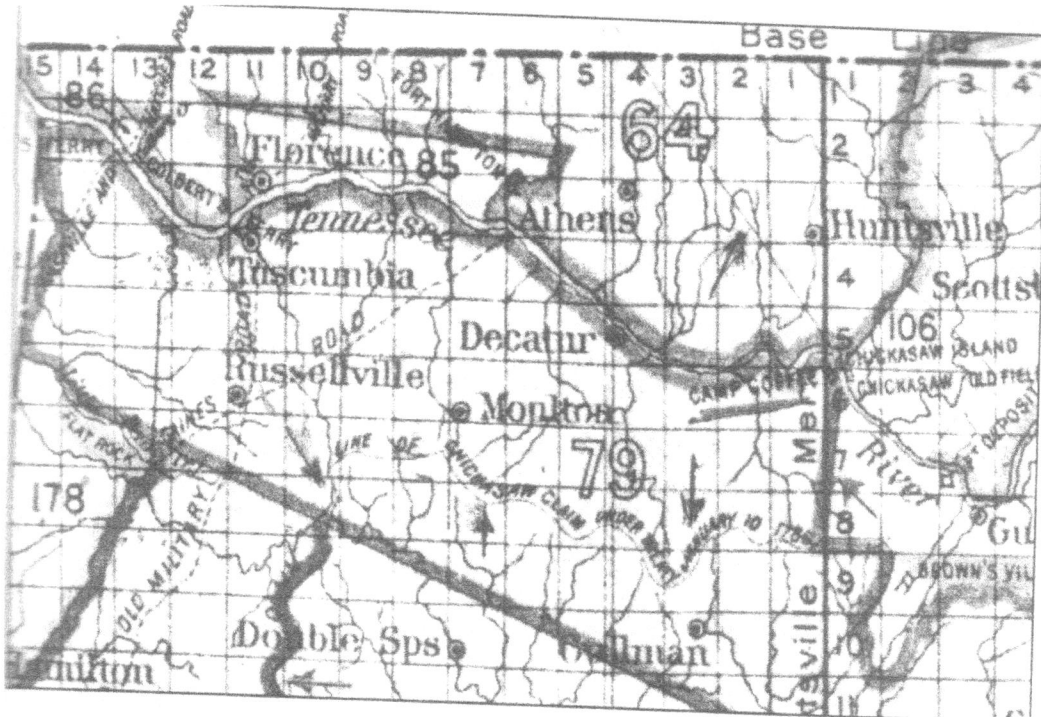

The Chickasaw Boundary of 1786 can be seen on this map along the Tennessee Divide, Source: Bureau of American Ethnology, 18th Annual Report

Warrior Mountains Indian Towns

Historic sites identified in the Tennessee Valley (Lawrence County) from the head of Elk River Shoals downstream to Big Muscle Shoals include Monee Town or Mouse Town, Doublehead's Town at Brown's Ferry, Fox's Stand, Melton's Bluff, Cuttatoy's Village, Gourd's Settlement (Courtland), and Shoal Town (Town Creek/Big Nance/Blue Water village). Doublehead's Chickamauga Confederacy established these towns starting in 1770; and, the towns were occupied by Lower Cherokees and other Chickamauga tribesmen until the Turkey Town Treaty of 1816.

Moneetown or Mouse Town

Monee Town or Mouse Town was an Indian village located north of the mountain at the mouth Fox's Creek in Lawrence County (Saunders, 1899). This Cherokee Indian village was located at the mouth of Fox's Creek near the present-day confluence with the Tennessee River. The Cherokee probably established Monee Town about 1770, shortly after the Chickasaws moved down the Tennessee River to Caney Creek. Monee Town was probably derived from the word "moneton" which in the Siouan linguistic family means "Big Water" people.

Swanton (1952) mentions a Cherokee town of Moneton in West Virginia and refers to the settlement as "a great town" which was later abandoned. The Cherokees that Ann Royall visited while in Lawrence County in 1818 were probably those that lived at or near Monee Town. Historical records indicate that Doublehead lived at the head of the shoals for some 12 years at or near Monee Town where the Brown's Ferry Landing was located in Lawrence County.

Some three miles easterly, from the head of Elk River Shoals at the junction of Fox's Creek and Tennessee River was the Cherokee Indian town of Monee Town or Mouse Town. This was the first Cherokee town beginning on the east edge of present-day Lawrence County and was our county's most upstream Cherokee town on the south side of the Tennessee River. The Indian village was located between Courtland and Decatur on Fox's Creek on the north side of Trinity Mountain.

According to a letter from Waco, Texas, May 9, 1882, and printed in The Moulton Advertiser on May 25, 1882, page 2, column 4, *"Lawrence was the banner County in Alabama in furnishing soldiers in the Texas struggle. Had not Dr. Shackleford and the Red Rovers been captured near Goliad, just after the fall of the Alamo, there would, doubtless, be many a veteran of that gallant band now living...Lawrence County still has her representatives in that band of patriots. I noticed... Aaron Burleson. The latter will be remembered by the old people who lived between Courtland and Decatur in the year 1817; if any such are now living. He was a brother of Gen. Ed Burleson of Texas Revolutionary fame. He was engaged in the killing of some Indians at **Mouse Town** on Foxe's Creek, east of Courtland in 1817, for which he fled the country, went to Missouri, thence to*

Texas. He has made many greasers as well as red skin bite the dust…He now lives in Bastrop, Bastrop County."

In another account, the Indian village is called Moneetown. *"James Burleson settled with his family on the north side of the mountain on Fox Creek. Here near an Indian village called **Monee Town**, the family became involved in a feud following an altercation between a son-in-law, Martin, and the Cherokees. After three of the Indians were slain, James Burleson and his son Edward fled to Missouri"* (Gentry, 1962).

In personal communication on December 18, 2003, Mr. Paul Ausbon and Mr. Bill Sams, whose ancestors lived on the river at Brown's Ferry, reported that Mouse Town was located at the junction of Fox Creek and the Tennessee River. Mr. Ausbon told me that he was born in 1925 and had known all his life of the Indian town that was called Mouse Town by his grandparent and parents. Both men told that the Mouse Town area was a favorite fishing location of their families. For years, the story of Mouse Town was passed down to Mr. Paul Ausbon. According to his grandparents, an Indian fight occurred at the old town site. They said the town was on the present-day Lawrence and Morgan County line, north of Trinity Mountain some two miles from Highway 20.

Rayford Hyatt (1993) gives the best description of the altercation between Burleson and the Cherokees as follows: *"The last Indian and white battle in present Lawrence County, of which we have found any record, occurred near Meltons Bluff (Mouse Town) in 1816. This indicates that some whites had already come into the area and were leasing farms from the Cherokee Indians.*

James Saunders, in 'Early Settlers,' writing many years later from oral tradition, says the fight occurred on Foxes Creek near a village called Monee Town when James Burleson and family killed three Cherokees and fled to Missouri. The 1820 census shows Burleson still in Lawrence County. This is the related Burlesons of later Texas fame.

In the 'National Intelligenser,' Washington, D.C., September 5, 1816, is given editorially the substance of a letter, dated August 13, 1816, to Col. Winston from James Burleson. It states in effect 'that he, Burleson, and others who had settled near Meltons Bluff (Mouse Town), on the south side of the Tennessee River to the number of eight men were attacked by a party of Cherokees armed with guns and war clubs, the number not known, on the night of the 11ᵗʰ inst. The whites resisted and three Indians were killed and one wounded. The fear of the Indians caused consternation among the settlers, and many moved away leaving promising crops.'

The 'Intelligenser' of September 10, 1816, from information at Huntsville dated August 17, 1816, enters further into details concerning the disturbance. "It seems that a Mr. Taylor had rented a field from some Cherokees. In his absence they offered some insult to Mrs. Taylor, who escaped to the home of her father, James Burleson. Burleson, Taylor and others went to the Indian settlement, where they found a number collected. They demanded an explanation. The Indians raised a yell and said fight. An attempt was made by the whites to cut them off from their arms. This produced a conflict.'"

Doublehead's Town

Doublehead's Town was located at Brown's Ferry near the head of Elk River Shoals. *"Yet, Doublehead was without influence or position until about the year 1790, when he established a town on the Tennessee River at the head of the Muscle Shoals. An early map of the Cherokee Country shows this village at a site near the south bank of Brown's Ferry below Athens. He later in 1802 moved it to the north bank of the river near the mouth of Blue Water Creek in Lauderdale County, Alabama... Inhabitants of Doublehead's Town, originally about 40 in number, were mostly cast-offs from other Cherokee and Creek villages. This motley bunch became infamous in Tennessee history as "The Ravagers of the Cumberlands"* (McDonald, 1989).

Historical records indicate that Doublehead lived in his Cherokee Indian town at Brown's Ferry from 1790 through December 1801. According to <u>History of Alabama</u> by Albert James Pickett (1851), *"Dec. 1801: Emigrants flocked to the Mississippi Territory...constructing flat-boats at Knoxville, they floated down the river to the head of the Muscle Shoals, where they disembarked at the house of Double-Head, a Cherokee Chief...placing their effects upon the horses, which had been brought down by land from Knoxville, they departed on foot for the Bigby settlements."* Based on this historical note, Doublehead was still living at

Brown's Ferry until 1802. The route immigrants utilized for bringing their horses to Brown's Ferry was no doubt portions of the South River Road.

In 1803, Patrick Wilson traveled along the southern side of the Tennessee River and followed the same route as the South River Road. The following excerpt describes the route along the South River Road, *"The expedition continued on the Natchez Trace to present day Alabama, here Wilson observed land controlled by the Chickamauga Cherokee, who…were highly resistant to territorial encroachment in the Tennessee Valley…At the Muscle Shoals… the expedition left the Natchez Trace to follow the south bank of the Tennessee River. Here the party rested in a Chickamauga Cherokee town (Doublehead's Town at Brown's Ferry) administered by Tal Tsuska (Doublehead), a controversial and historically significant chief who controlled transportation routes… continuing in Cherokee territory, Wilson's party traveled north, passing through "Watts or Wills Town"… Wilson's narrative ends in Hiwasee; a Cherokee town no longer in existence"* (Hathorn and Sabino, 2001). By the time of Wilson's expedition in 1803, Doublehead had already moved from Brown's Ferry to the Shoal Town area on the north side of the river near Blue Water Creek.

Doublehead's Town at Brown's Ferry was also known for a brief period as Cox's Ferry. A man by the name of Cox, who was supposedly the son of Zechariah Cox, had apparently married one of the Brown Cherokee girls and briefly called the area Cox's Ferry. Some two miles west of the Indian village, the Brown's Ferry Road intersected Black Warriors' Path and the South River Road.

Doublehead's Town was on the south bank of the Tennessee River at river miles 293 and 294. The town site lay between present-day Mallard Creek Campground and the old Brown's Ferry Road. Doublehead's home was thought to be on a point just downstream from the ferry location but within sight of the old river crossing. Doublehead ran a house of entertainment that catered to all kind of needs of travelers. It is said that he was very generous to allow two older ladies, both of whom had a bunch of girls, to live in his house. Many have speculated that Doublehead's entertainment probably included many types of mischief. Doublehead had learned very rapidly about making money from his mixed-blood friends. One such business partner was Captain John D. Chisholm.

Today, you can walk over the fields along the old river bank and find plenty of evidence of a large, extensive, and historic dwelling site. Old nails are in abundance along with pieces of glassware, historic pottery, slave made bricks, and even a large area of garlic, buttercups, and other plants that indicate historic occupation. In particular, the garlic grows on a small knoll just a few hundred yards from the ferry site. We refer to this knoll as Doublehead's home site and the plants as Doublehead's garlic. His garlic has been transplanted to the Oakville Indian Mounds Park. Remains of chert projectile points indicate prehistoric Indian occupation as early as the Archaic Period; therefore, Doublehead's Town site was used for thousands of years by native people.

Melton's Bluff

Melton's Bluff was established by an Irishman, John Melton, his Cherokee wife Ocuma, and her Cherokee family at the head of the Elk River Shoals on the south side of the Tennessee River in Lawrence County. Ocuma was the youngest sister of Doublehead; and therefore, Doublehead and John Melton were brother-in-laws. Prior to white settlement in Lawrence County, Melton's Cherokee family first raided keelboats and later, after the area became more civilized, guided keelboats through the Shoals. After the Cherokee and Chickasaw gave up their land in 1817, Marathon was established in 1818 by Andrew Jackson and his associates near the site of Melton's Bluff.

Melton's Bluff was approximately seven miles west of Brown's Ferry; the site was also a prehistoric town located on the west side of Jack's Slough, at Tennessee River mile 288.5. The site contains a large ceremonial Indian mound covering over one acre and stands some fifteen to twenty feet high. In addition approximately one hundred feet from the Tennessee River, a small snail mound is located between the large mound and the present river bank. During historic occupation by the Cherokee Indians, the site west of the mounds for about one mile became known as Melton's Bluff, named after an Irishman, John Melton. Melton's Bluff was a historic Cherokee Town that was purchased by General Andrew Jackson from half-blood Cherokee David Melton on November 22, 1816 (McDonald, William Lindsey, 1989). At Melton's Bluff located between Tennessee River miles 287 and 288.5, the South River Road continued west while Black Warriors' Path turned north, crossed the river, and passed Fort Hampton, Bridgewater, Elkton, and on to the French Lick.

In <u>Letters from Alabama 1817-1822</u> by Anne Newport Royall is a description of a route to Melton's Bluff from Florence as follows: *"Melton's Bluff, January 8th, 1818... I was three days on the road to this place. Melton's Bluff is at the head of Mussel Shoals...I went direct to the foot of the Shoals, 70 miles from Huntsville, crossed the river, and come upon the south side of Tennessee River...three miles in width! the largest body of water that I ever saw. It was at this time very high and muddy; and the noise produced by the water washing over the rocks was tremendous... we saw a boat hung on a rock, about the middle of the stream...I took a guide, one of the pilots, and crossed the river next morning, in a ferry boat...upon leaving the ferry... I was to pass by several Indian farms... About ten o'clock we came in sight of the first Indian farm... you cross Town Creek in a canoe and swim your horses; this will cost you one dollar...I, with my horses, were safely on the other side... Rhea (my guide's name) said I had two more creeks to pass... however, these were easily forded...Rhea... had piloted boats through the Muscle Shoals, fifteen years; sometimes four at a time, at ten dollars each. He sails down one day, and walks back to the next... this land is so clear of undergrowth that you may drive a wagon anywhere through the woods...we passed many Indian houses in the day, and some beautiful springs. Melton's Bluff is a town, and takes its name from...John Melton...Irishman by birth...attached himself to the Cherokee Indians... Melton's Bluff... a very large plantation of cotton and maize, worked by about sixty slaves and owned by General Jackson, who bought the interest of old Melton."*

This firsthand account in January 1818 of Ms. Royall confirms the existence of a road, which still had Indian houses standing, along the south bank of the Tennessee River. The Cherokee and Chickasaw Indians had given up the land in September 1816 approximately fifteen months prior to Ms. Royall's visit to Melton's Bluff. The route of the South River Road was clearly established and had been in existence for some time.

The following portion of a story on Melton's Bluff by Rayford Hyatt (1993) gives details on the Indian village. *"The place was named for a white man, Melton, who settled there probably as a trader, married a Cherokee woman, thereby becoming a member of the Cherokee Nation. James Saunders in 'Early Settlers' says his name was James Melton. Anne Royall in 'Letters From*

Alabama' says he was John. A Cherokee Treaty of 1806 ceding lands north of the Tennessee River exempted a tract 2 by 3 miles to Moses Melton and Charles Hicks in equal shares. Oliver D. Street in a paper on 'The Indians of Marshall County' says that Meltonsville of Marshall County was named for Charles Melton, an old man of Herculean frame who once lived at Meltons Bluff. Whichever he was, the others were probably his sons.

Meltons Bluff was located at the head of the Muscle Shoals in the SE 1/4 - SE 1/4 Sec 25 T3S R7W. Most of the buildings were in a line on top of the bluff. Anne Royall in 'Letters from Alabama' who stayed at the Bluff for a long period in 1818-19 says Melton got started by robbing flat boats coming down the river. It is more likely that Indians did the robbing and he traded for the slaves and goods. He also for many years furnished river pilots to boats through the Muscle Shoals for a fee with the pilots walking back to the Bluff from Florence.

In 1774 a settlement party of 15 whites and 21 slaves from South Carolina led by William Scott, were descending the Tennessee by flat boat to Natchez when they were attacked at the head of Muscle Shoals by a number of Cherokees under The Bowle. All of the white people were killed, and the slaves and goods taken. The Cherokee tribe disavowed the act of The Bowle and his followers who, fearing capture and punishment, fled to the west and located on the Arkansas River and with subsequent additions to their settlement they remained there many years.

In later years, Melton seemed to operate in a profitable legal manner. Besides houses of entertainment and boating activities at the Bluff, he owned large cotton and corn plantations on both sides of the river. There were numerous travelers down the river. Goods came down by flatboat from the Watauga settlement bound for New Orleans. Settlers from Virginia and Carolina crossed the mountains and descended by boat, some bound for the lower Mississippi and others for the lower Tombigbee. Those bound for the latter stopped at the bluff, travelled by horseback to Cotton Gin Port, built more boats and descended. Those going on downstream sometimes had to lay over a long time at the Bluff waiting for a rise in the river to get over the Shoals.

In 'Letters from Alabama', Anne Royal states that Melton had removed across the river in present Limestone County and died there about 1815 in old age. General Andrew Jackson leased his Melton's Bluff plantation. It consisted of cotton lands, about 60 slaves and an overseer who lived in Melton's old log house of two stories, located a short distance from the village. General Jackson had trouble with his overseers and fugitive slaves, and was an anxious absentee landlord.

In 1818 the village stretched along the top of the bluff, consisted of two large houses of entertainment, several doctors, one hatters shop, one warehouse, and several mechanics. Living there were ten permanent families. There were a lot of travelers there at this time looking at lands and waiting for the coming land sales.

Melton's Bluff village died out soon after the land sales in the fall of 1818. All lands in present Lawrence County became the property of the United States and had to be purchased from it. The first event that then occurred at Melton's Bluff was a failed attempt to set up the city of Marathon, apparently by General Andrew Jackson, General John Coffey, and other speculators. The town was surveyed into blocks and lots by Coffey, who was then surveyor general; and the town was almost a mile square and located at and west of Melton's Bluff. A few of the 556 lots were sold with a down payment, but all were relinquished, and there is no evidence any buildings went up.

A block in the center of Marathon was set aside as a public square, so there may have been hope that it would be selected as county seat. Moulton was selected, and it and Courtland built quickly into towns, and this may have caused the downfall of Marathon. The former site of Melton's Bluff is now TVA property, and Marathon is a part of the Wheeler Plantation."

Cuttyatoy's Village

The fourth downstream Indian town from the head of the Muscle Shoals connected by the South River Road was Cuttyatoy's Village. The village was actually on Gilchrist Island at the western end of Elk River Shoals near the south bank of the Tennessee River. According to the <u>American Whig Review</u>, Volume 15, Issue 87, March 1852, page 247: *"Colonel (Joseph) Brown…a participant in the battle of Talledega (November 9, 1813)…met Charles Butler… and learned from him that…Chief Cuttyatoy, was still alive…he was then living on an island in the Tennessee River, near the mouth of Elle (Elk) River, and that he had with him several Negroes ... taken by him at Nickajack on the 9ᵗʰ of May, 1788... with ten picked men, Brown proceeded to the island, went to the head man's (Cuttyatoy) lodge and exhibited to him General (Andrew) Jackson's order, and demanded that Cuttyatoy's Negroes be immediately sent over to Fort Hampton...In crossing the river, Colonel Brown and his men took up the Negroes, and Cuttyatoy's wife behind them, to carry them over the water while the Indian men crossed on a raft (Brown's Ferry) higher up (stream)."* Cuttyatoy and his men utilized the South River Road to reach Brown's Ferry. Colonel Joseph Brown and his men reached Fort Hampton that morning while Cuttyatoy and his men arrived in the afternoon.

Today, Cuttyatoy's Village is under the backwaters created by Wheeler Dam. The old Indian town site lies buried below the surface of Wheeler Lake, as are most of the river villages that were located on islands of Elk River Shoals. Between the mouth of Spring Creek on the south side and Elk River on the north side of the Tennessee River, the islands of Elk River Shoals are under some twenty feet or more of water. It was between these islands of the Elk River Shoals that General Joe Wheeler's cavalry crossed the Tennessee River on October 9, 1863.

Gourd's Settlement (Courtland)

The Town of Courtland was laid out on the site of Gourd's Settlement, a Cherokee town, and was surrounded by old-fields on which Indians cabins were still standing when the first white settlers arrived (Saunders, 1899). Courtland was on the banks of Big Nance Creek about 5 miles south of the river at a trail crossing on Big Nance. The site was along the Sipsie Trail that connected the French Lick (Nashville) to Tuscaloosa.

The fifth downstream Indian town from the head of Muscle Shoals was a Cherokee village called Gourd's Settlement which was at the present-day town of Courtland. On December 28, 1807, Captain Edmund Pendleton Gaines made this note on his survey from Melton's Bluff to Cotton Gin Port: *"8ᵗʰ mile.... At 119 chains, Cross the path which leads from the Shoal Town, eastwardly, to the* **Goard's Settlement**, *about 3 miles distance"* (Stone, James H., 1971). Based on Gaines measurements of some 8.7 miles westerly from Melton's Bluff, then easterly for three miles, Gourd's settlement was in the center of present-day

Courtland, Alabama. Eventually, three Indian roads intersected at Gourd's Settlement: the Gaines' Trace, the South River Road, and the Sipsie Trail, which later became the Cheatham Road or portions of present-day Highway 33.

Gourd's Settlement was obviously named after a Cherokee Indian man called Gourd. According to *Letters from Alabama 1817-1822* written by Anne Royall on January 12, 1818, page 131, is the following: *"Guide says Gourd was very kind; he knew him for fifteen years. He helped subdue the Creeks, and made an excellent soldier."* Anne Royall described Gourd's log house as being on the west side of Town Creek, ten years after Gaines' account; however, she wrote her letter after the fact and might have been wrong on the exact location; furthermore, Gaines was a surveyor and made precise measurements and locations.

Gourd's Town was at the junction of the South River Road and the Sipsie Trail, an early Indian route from Tuscaloosa to the French Lick (Nashville, Tennessee). Also a prehistoric village containing an Indian mound was located at the site on the banks of Path Killer Creek which later became known as Big Nance. According to Captain Edmund Pendleton Gaines on December 27, 1807, *"we proceeded, same course...6th mile...At 116 [chains] (west of Melton's Bluff) Path Killer's Creek, 3 chains wide from tops of banks"* (Stone, 1971). In 1807 when Captain Gaines identified Path Killer Creek (named after Cherokee Chief Path Killer), he was traveling portions of the South River Road but was intent on surveying a line from Melton's Bluff on the Tennessee River to Cotton Gin Port on the Tombigbee River; therefore, he basically followed the Old Chickasaw Trail to the heart of the Chickasaw Nation.

According to a February, 1829 Lawrence County court record, *"a road from Gourd Landing on the Tennessee River to intersect the road from Courtland to Lamb's Ferry at or near Gordon's fence the nearist and best way... Order, 1829, Jury of Review of a road from Courtland to Gourds."* This road either crossed or followed portions of both the Sipsie Trail and Gaines Trace.

Shoal Town

Shoal Town was a large Cherokee settlement was located at the mouth of Town Creek and extended a mile along the river and far up the creek (Leftwich,

1935). The town was abandoned in 1808 when some 1130 Cherokees left the area with Tahlontuskee for lands in Arkansas.

Shoal Town was on Big Muscle Shoals and connected by the South River Road and Doublehead's Trace was located between Blue Water Creek and Town Creek on the Tennessee River. Shoal Town was the home of Talohuskee Benge, the half-brother to Sequoyah. Later, Talohuskee's great uncle Doublehead moved to the Shoal Town area about 1802. Shoal Town was located some six miles from the eastern end of Big Muscle Shoals; in Captain Edmund Pendleton Gaines survey on December 28, 1807, he notes the following, *"8th mile... at 119 chains. Cross the path (South River Road) which leads from **Shoal-Town**, eastwardly, to the Goards Settlement (Courtland), about 3 miles distance"* (Stone, 1971).

Shoal Town was considered the largest Cherokee Indian village in the Big Bend of the Tennessee River. At the location, the Blue Water Ferry crossed the river from the eastern side of the mouth of Blue Water Creek to the western side of the mouth of Path Killer's Creek. Talohuskee Benge, son of Doublehead's niece, Wurteh Watts and trader John Benge, lived at Shoal Town with Doublehead and probably operated the ferry, a common practice at large Cherokee River Towns.

*"Both the French and the English contended for the Indian trade along the western waters; the French planted a post at Muscle Shoals before 1715. Because of the increasing importance of trade with the whites the Cherokees planted villages near the Muscle Shoals area in the last quarter of the eighteenth century. There was Doublehead's village on the Tennessee and **a large settlement (Shoal Town) at the mouth of Town Creek, extending a mile along the river and far up the creek"*** (Leftwich, 1935). The Cherokee village described above is Shoal Town, which was located on Big Muscle Shoals of the Tennessee River between Big Nance (Path Killer's) Creek, Town Creek, and Blue Water Creek.

While living at Shoal Town, Doublehead requested help from the U.S. Government; however, he was no stranger to the government when asking for help, money, or handouts. This particular incident is recorded in Henry T. Malone's (1956) book *Cherokees of the Old South*:

"A scarcity of corn caused by a drought in the Cherokee Nation during the year 1804 was a crisis which Meigs faced in his typical fashion. The first request for food came from **Doublehead** *and other Cherokees in the Muscle Shoals area on the Lower Tennessee River. The Agent immediately sent them three hundred bushels of corn, for which the Indians paid $110. Meigs, however, requested and received permission from the War Department to return the money; he thought it his duty 'to give the necessary relief — believing that humanity and interest combine to make it proper especially when interesting negotiations with them are now soon to be opened.' Meigs' policy pleased his government. Henry Dearborn sent him the President's congratulations, urging Meigs to continue helping needy Indians: 'You will embrace so favorable an opportunity for impressing the minds of the Cherokees with the fatherly concern and attention of the President to the distresses of his red children.'"*

Today, Doublehead's Resort is located in Lawrence County, Alabama, at the site of Shoal Town. The resort is a modern facility catering to thousands of people each year and is located on the east bank of Town Creek near where it empties into the Tennessee River. The resort area extends up the river toward Big Nance Creek and has become a popular tourist site. Along the bank of Town Creek are numerous two-story cabins which can accommodate entire families. Each cabin has a water-front dock which provides boating facilities for resort visitors. The resort also boasts a lodge, swimming facilities, horseback riding, and many other accommodations that make for a pleasurable stay. If Doublehead were alive today, he would have to be proud of the facility at his old homesite that bears his name; therefore, the legends of Doublehead live on at this beautiful recreational facility in the county his descendants still call home.

1818 Witness to the Indians of the Warrior Mountains

Anne Royall provides the first in-depth report of Indian life in Lawrence County in January 1818. She seems surprised the Indian people during this period of time lived and dressed like white settlers. Even though she does not describe the Indian people as savages, she infers they are an inferior race when compared to white people. She finally comes to the conclusion that the Cherokees were more advanced in civilization than she first imagined. *"By all that I have said in regard to these Cherokees, you may perceive they are far advanced in civilized arts and manners"* (Royall, 1818).

Anne Royall described the area around the Shoals and Melton's Bluff. *"The Tennessee River is wider at the foot of the Shoals than the Ohio. Except at the. "Bluff" (steep ledges of rock) the land at the sides of the river are lowlands which are often inundated by high water. Land surrounding the river appears to be undulating; alternately elevated or depressed like waves."*

The Indian farms were described by Anne Royall: *"Cornfields, apple orchards, and peach orchards occupied the lands. Fences, four or five rails high, provided enclosures. The houses of the Indians in this area were cabins built very much like those of the white people. The cabins were roomy and tightly built. The logs were round, very light, and laid close upon each other. The door was as high as a common door, but only half as wide."*

Melton's Bluff, settled by an Irishman named John Melton, was located at the head of Elk River Shoals on the Tennessee River. John Melton, with the help of the Indians, robbed boats coming down the river, murdered the crews, and stole their slaves. After a peace treaty was signed with the Indians in 1806, Melton lived quietly on a farm and later ran a house of entertainment (Royall, 1819).

A description of the Indians and their lifestyles was given by Anne Royall. She describes the Cherokee women as having "nothing majestic or dignified" about them. The women have no "expression of countenance-they have a dead eye." They were ugly lumps of things-short and thick. The hair of the Cherokee woman was jet black and very coarse, like a horse's mane. The women wore their hair parted from the crown of the head to its termination on the forehead and clubbed in the back with a blue or red ferret. The color of the Cherokee is that of dark mulattoes. Many were mixed-blood (offspring of white and Indian) but were as unsociable as the others. The hands and feet of the women were very small and beautiful.

The dress of the Cherokee women was much like that of a white woman. Their dressed were well--made with fine cotton shawls on the shoulders.

Many of the women wore men's hats' there were no bonnets. They had good shoes or moccasins on their feet. They wore hundreds of beads around their neck. The dress of the Cherokee men was as fashionable as that of the women. The men wore "very neat half-boots" and broadcloth coats. Good hats were worn though some men preferred tying handkerchiefs around their heads because it was more convenient for hunting.

A day in the life of Cherokees in the process of being removed was described by Anne Royall. The camps contained about three hundred Indians. Cooking was done over fires built having forks of wood driven into the ground, a stick laid across it, had a pot in which meat boiled hung from the stick. Most of the men hunted with rifles. In the camp, several men were skinning and preparing meat (probably venison).

The Cherokee infants were strapped onto their mother's back with blankets. The women went through the different vocations of pounding corn into meal, carrying wood and water, and sewing. Parched corn was pounded into meal using a pestle.

The meal was light brown in color and pounded until it was coarse in texture. This meal was not used to make bread but was mixed with water for drinking purposes.

Early Indian Trails and Roads

The earliest roads were Indian trails or paths through the wilderness. Most of these trails and paths could be followed on foot or horseback but were not suitable for coaches or wagons. These Indian paths became important to white settlements and white development of the North Alabama area.

Some of these trails extended all the way across. Alabama. There were a great many short trails and hunting trails, but there were fewer long trails. These trails were determined by the lay of the land. Many of today's highways and railroad lines follow these early trails.

The Buffalo Trail through the Bankhead National Forest

The High Town Path was an example of a long Indian trail that passed through Lawrence County. This trial was named for the Cherokee village of High Town in present-day Etowah County, Georgia (Summers ell, 1981). The High Town trail extended from the recent site of Atlanta, Georgia, westward through the Cherokee Nation south of Sand Mountain, through the Creek Nation, and into the Chickasaw Nation. The trail passed through the present counties of Lawrence, Franklin, and Marion in Alabama prior to entering Mississippi.

The Ancient Indian Trail of the High Town Path

      The High Town or Ridge Path ran in an east-west direction along the mountain ridges avoiding lowlands and creek crossings: The path followed the continental divide through Lawrence County and into Mississippi. The Leola Road and Ridge Road in Lawrence County represent the most accurate route of the High Town Path through Lawrence County. The High Town Path was listed as the boundary of the Chickasaw Nation. The Little Okfuskee-Chickasaw Nation Path, from the Chattahoochee River through Little Okfuskee and Flat Rock, joined the High Town Path and lead to Copper Town in the Chickasaw Nation. A fork of the path left from Eastport across the western part of Colbert County where Russellville is now.

Gaines' Trace was apparently the first white settler road through the Warrior Mountains and began at Melton's Bluff in Lawrence County, Alabama. The trace ran from Melton's Bluff north of present-day Courtland through the southern part of Colbert County to Cotton, Gin Port at the head of navigation on the Tombigbee River. About 1805, General George Strothers Gaines directed the opening of the road.

Black Warrior's Path and Sipsie Trail are also important North-South Indian routes through Lawrence County, Alabama.

In October 1801, a treaty between the U.S. and the Chickasaws gave permission to cut and open a wagon road between Nashville, Tennessee and Natchez, Mississippi. In 1806, Congress appropriated $6,000 for opening the road. The road known as the Natchez Trace, passed through Colbert and Lauderdale Counties in North Alabama. Under the treaty, the Indians reserved rights to establish public uses of entertainment along the route and to control the necessary courses (Gentry, 1962).

Warrior Mountains Mixed-Blood Indians

According to Wright (1951), white traders and their employees settled and married among the Cherokees, Chickasaws, and Creeks in the late 1600's and early 1700's. By the beginning of the 1800's, these Indian Nations were controlled by mixed-blood families, who became prominent in Southeastern Indian history. The mixed blood Indians of the Warrior Mountains were usually of Scots-Irish or Scottish decent.

According to the Alabama Indian Affairs Commission brochure, there has been some 500 years in which the Indian community interacted with white settlers through intermarriage. Documented mixing of blood lines of whites and Indians in Lawrence County cover over 250 years of our local history. Probably over forty percent of the old families who settled Lawrence County during the early 1800's are mixed-blood (Scots-Irish and Indian) descendants. Today, several of our school children are certified members of the Echota Cherokee Tribe.

Ella Allred and John Norman Minor, half-blood Cherokees

Following Indian trails and roads, the first Europeans came into this area during the late 1600's. These people were probably fur traders, prospectors, and farmers who were seeking their fortune in Alabama Indian Country. The first white people were mostly men of Irish or Scottish descent. According to Daniels (1962), many European men preferred the Indian girls to white women.

Aunt Jenny Brooks (1/2 Cherokee)

The Indian women were described as dusky maidens with flashing eyes, voluptuous forms, delicate hands and feet, raven hair and a merry laugh. Early travelers in Tennessee wrote of the Cherokee beauties that had features formed cheerful and friendly (Daniels, 1962). In the 1700's, many white men came into this area, married Indians and made the Warrior Mountains of North Alabama their home.

Straud Riddle, ¾ Cherokee. Killed last Timber wolf in Warrior Mountains

One of the first white persons recorded in this area was a Scotsman, James Logan Colbert, in 1729 (Gibson, 1971). Colbert came to this area with a group of

English traders. Colbert joined the Chickasaw Indians and married three Chickasaws who bore him many children. His sons, William, George, Levi, Samuel, Joseph, and James, were the principal Chickasaw to fight with the Americans against the French.

Many of these people made their homes in the Tennessee Valley and mountain region to the south. James Logan Colbert became very rich owning 150 Negro slaves and set the economic and social tone for the growing mixed blood settlements which separated themselves more and more from the primitive full bloods (Gibson, 1971).

John Melton came into Lawrence County around the 1780's with the Cherokee Indians. Melton, an Irishman by birth, married a Cherokee and died at a large farm on the north side of Tennessee River in about 1815 (Harris, 1977). Melton owned farms on both sides of the Tennessee River and also owned a great number of slaves. In the latter part of his life, he became alarmed from the threats of the Creeks and moved from Lawrence County to the north side of the river.

Mary Alice Thornton, a Cherokee, Lamar Marshall's great grandmother, and John Nelson Shaw ¾ Cherokee.

Melton had several children by his Indian wife, Ocuma-a sister of Doublehead, most of whom married white people (Royall, 1818). Many whites coming into North Alabama in the 1700's made friends with the' Indians and married their young women. This is thought to be the case because other whites who later came here to settle found many inhabitants to be of mixed blood (Thompson, 1968). Many Cherokee Indians in the Tennessee Valley (Lawrence County) were of mixed blood; the offspring of a white and an Indian.

In order to forestall removal with the Compact of 1802, progressive Cherokee leaders, many of whom were mixed bloods, undertook an ambitious and aggressive program that would replace ancient Cherokee culture with that of the educated and Christianized white man (Woodward, 1963). Remarkable advancement of the Cherokee as a people came about largely through the influence of the mixed-blood families of Irish, German, English, Welsh or Scottish descent, whose ancestors settled and married in the Nation during the Eighteenth century (Wright, 1951). During Indian Removal, mixed blood inhabitants were allowed to remain in North Alabama because they were married to whites or were able to identify themselves with white ancestry (Thompson, 1968).

Bob White and Evie Sims White (3/4 Cherokee)

The majority of Warrior Mountains' Indian children and their parents, if asked the question of race, would probably not reply Indian even though they are proud of their Indian ancestry. Due to Indian removal and intermarriage, Warrior Mountains' Indian people became thoroughly absorbed into the general population. Diluted Indian blood lines occurred because of isolation from other full blood Indian people cause by the Indian removal during the early 1800's. Intermarriage with non-Indian people was an effective method to prevent removal from their homeland to hostile unknown lands west of the Mississippi River.

Jane Parker Smith, ½ Cherokee, and Kay C. McVay, ½ Cherokee and Savannah Brannon

Fearing not only for their personal property but also their lives, the remaining Indian people in the Warrior Mountains denied their race, held to white man's ways, and almost completely lost their Indian culture and heritage. Some Indian people with dark complexions claimed to be Black Dutch or Black Irish. Most claimed some European Nationality in denying their Indian heritage.

Many were told why their grandmothers and great-grandmothers had only first names and why records of birth did not exist. They were also told how the

Indian blood line passed from generation to generation. Since Indian removal, the degree of Indian blood of the Warrior Mountains' people has steadily diminished and will continue to do so throughout future generations. With the passage of the Civil Rights Acts of 1968, many mixed-blood Indian descents began to seek and reclaim their Indian heritage, but for many it was too late.

William Sims (½ Cherokee) and Mary Davidson (Full Cherokee) are the parents of Evie Sims White.

Presently, about 20% of north Alabama's school children are state recognized Indians of mixed blood. Warrior Mountains' mixed-blood school children have mostly Cherokee and Creek blood lines. Many of north west Alabama's Indian people are Cherokee mixed bloods who migrated here from the east part of Alabama, the Carolinas, and Georgia in the early 1800's.

Today, some of these mixed blood Indian children who attend public schools in north Alabama are listed as white children. The majority of the Indian children in the Warrior Mountains are from 1/8 to 1/64 Indian blood. The Indian students in Lawrence County receive instruction in the cultural heritage of Southeastern Indians which is integrated into the regular public school curriculum under the direction of the Indian Education Program.

Most of the mixed blood Indian children in north Alabama belong to the Echota Cherokee Tribe. Jane Weeks, past Executive Director of the Alabama Indian Affairs Commission, has summed up the situation quite well, *"In all the many hundreds of years in which the Indian Community has interacted with the European community who came to this new and wonderful country, through intermarriage many of our people are not likely to "look" Indian and because their "blood quantum" has diminished it does not diminish their ethnic pride or rights"* (Weeks, 1988).

Kinlock Rock Shelter was utilized by prehistoric and historic Indian people of the Warrior Mountains.

Indian Lifestyles of the Warrior Mountains

Introduction

The lifestyles of the Warrior Mountain Indians, including the Cherokee, Creek and Chickasaw, were closely related. Food, clothing, weapons and homes were similar due to geographic location and climate, but, each tribe had its own unique characteristics.

The coming of the Europeans drastically changed lifestyles of our Indian people; cloth replaced buckskin; metal tools replaced stone tools; log cabins replaced clay daubed houses. Agriculture became the main occupation. Many of the ways of the white man became the ways to the Indian man. Eventually these tribes became known as the "Civilized" tribes.

Cherokee Lifestyle

The Cherokee, who are among the oldest inhabitants of the United States, entered Alabama about the 1750's. Because of the later contact with white traders and soldiers the Cherokee way of life changed greatly. Before European contact, the Cherokees made their own weapons. The main hunting weapon was the bow and arrow. The bow was usually made from sycamore, hickory, or ash; but the favorite was black locust or honey locust. The bow was a little over three feet depending on the man's height. It was broad flat and tapered toward both ends. The bow did not have a carved hand grip. Both ends were notched to hold the bow string. Bear guts were considered the best material for the bow string.

Arrows were made primarily from mountain cane. The Indians used red dogwood or other wood for arrows when cane was not available. Arrows were about two and one-half feet long. Points were made of copper, bones, chert (flint), or by simply sharpening the ends of the shaft. Sinew was secured with glue made from boiled deer hooves. Bear grease was applied frequently to protect the bow from dampness.

The blowgun was another Cherokee weapon. The blowgun was made from a piece of cane cut to a length of seven to nine feet. The cane was hollowed out by dropping hot coals into the cane. Another method was to sharpen a piece of cane, apply wet sand to the point, and use a rotating motion to drill a hole through each joint.

The blowgun darts were made of hardwood splinter. Blowgun darts were ten to twelve inches long. Darts had several inches of thistle down or animal hair tied to one end to form an air seal in the cane. The Cherokees were accurate up to sixty feet with the blowgun. The blowgun was used primarily for small game such as rabbit, squirrel, turkey or birds; but, larger game was killed by being shot in the eye with the blow gun. There is no evidence that Cherokees used poison on the points.

Cherokees lived in villages. The Cherokee never lived in teepees, but built permanent homes in small villages. Villages were built close to an abundant water supply and forest. The houses were clustered together and surrounded by fields and pastures. The villages were laid out around a central plaza.

The council house was the center of the plaza. The council house was the largest structure in the village. The council house had seven sides-one for each of the seven clans. At council meetings, clans sat in their designated areas. The council house served as the religious as well as political center of the town. Important matters were discussed publicly. A sacred fire was burned in the center of the council house.

Seven open sheds were across the plaza from the council house. These sheds served as council areas for the seven clans during the hot summer months. The sheds were built around a circle that held a sacred fire. Dwelling houses and storage houses were built around the plaza area to protect the Council.

The Cherokee house or ge-tsa'di had walls constructed of upright saplings imbedded closely together in the ground. Smaller branches were woven around the saplings. A mixture of clay and grass was used to plaster the walls. The roof was covered with bark or' thinly split wood shingles. The door, which was the only opening except for the small hole in the roof, was about two feet wide.

Wooden platforms, about two feet above the floor and covered with cane mats and animal skins, served as both couches and beds.

Tuchee (Cherokee) by George Catlin

The winter house or the asi' had walls built of logs standing on end and woven together with white oak strips that made solid walls. The roof was cone shaped. White oak splints were used to make the roofs. A clay mixture was used to plaster the inside and outside of the house which was covered with bark or grass. A fire burned in the center of the rooms with beds lining the walls. The door of the winter house was about four feet high, and it was so narrow that only one person could enter at a time. A small peephole was level with the ground so the enemies could be seen. Cherokee houses were filled with smoke; therefore, they slept with their head in deerskin to avoid breathing it. Winter houses continued to be used well into the nineteenth century.

Summer houses underwent a change in the mid-eighteenth century. Europeans introduced metal tools and new building techniques. Log construction techniques were brought to North America by German immigrants. Beams were interlocked at the corners by notching. Whites as well as Cherokees used this structure as a model for the architecture of all the inhabitants of the Warrior Mountains region.

The Cherokees had several recognizable physical characteristics. The Cherokees' skin was lighter than other Indians because their homes were in dense forests and mountainous areas and thus had less sun exposure. In addition, it is thought that the Cherokees intermarried with the Welsh who came over with Prince Madoc in 1100. During early settlement days, the Cherokee intermarried with Scots-Irish, Scots, and other settlers.

Cherokee men plucked or pulled all the hair from their bodies except for their eye brows, and a narrow crest on their heads. The crest began at the crown of the head, where it measured about two inches wide, and stood upright. The crest was long-at the neck-line and was often decorated with quills, beads, or a single feather. Cherokee men were the tallest of all Southeastern Indians. They were well built with strong muscular legs. Cherokee women had long black hair that usually hung to the waist. These women parted their hair in the middle. The hair was bound with deerskin thongs or it was braided.

Cherokee men and women wore jewelry and used tattooing as adornment. Men liked to wear necklaces showing, like trophies, that they had been successful in war or hunting. Elk teeth and bear claws were also used for this purpose. Earrings and bracelets were worn to signify victory. Tattooing was common among Cherokee men. Tattooing was used as a mark of personal identification. Designs of animal figures, serpent, stars, the moon, the sun, and scrolls were used. Designs were made by pricking the skin with a sharp object, like a garfish tooth, bone or needle. Tattooing was to designate honors.

Cherokee men wore three different articles of clothing. The breechcloth was a strip of skin or cloth about 6 feet long and 1 foot wide. The breech cloth was worn between the legs and looped over the belt the waist. The breech cloth's ends hung down in front and back to the knees. Cherokee men wore buckskin leggings as protection from the underbrush and from the cold in winter. The leggings were made in pairs, but were not sewn together. They fitted the whole length of the leg and were held up by a cord tied to the waist string. A jacket made of buckskin, reaching to the knees, was also worn; in cold weather, a bearskin or blanket was thrown around the shoulders.

The main item of clothing for Cherokee women was short, deerskin skirt hanging to the knees. Today Cherokee women wear tear dresses as tribal regalia. The dress is made from cotton with a small floral sign. The dress is trimmed with bright ribbons or diamond design appliquéd to the fabric. Today Cherokee men wear shirts decorated with brightly colored ribbons.

Like other Southeastern Indians, the Cherokee food supply depended upon their environment. Cherokee survival depended on an ample food supply. The Cherokee raised crops of beans, pumpkins, squash, and most importantly, corn. Wild grapes, persimmons, plums, blackberries, mushrooms, chestnuts, walnuts, hickory nuts, acorns, and wild greens were many of the plant foods that were gathered. Cherokees hunted deer, wild turkey, bear, squirrel, rabbit and quail. Deer was the main source of meat and hides. When a Cherokee hunter killed a deer, he always asked its spirit for pardon.

Rivers and streams yielded a bountiful supply of fish, turtle, and mussels. Fishermen used bone hooks and lines. Nets, traps and spears were used to catch fish.

Cherokees cooked their food in a variety of different ways to prepare it for eating. Boiling was the most common method of cooking with different foods combined to make a thick stew. Bread, and sometimes meat, was baked by wrapping the food in cornhusks or leaves and covering it with hot coals. Meat was also often cut into small pieces and broiled over an open fire. The Cherokees used common food preservation methods. Drying was the most common preservation method. Corn could be stored on the cob. Beans were dried in the pod or shelled. Pumpkins and squash were cut into strips and put in the sun to dry. Meat was dried over the fire. Cherokees also smoked their meats to preserve them (Hudson, 1976).

Cherokee religious beliefs were based upon nature. The Sun, the source of the warmth, light, and life, was one of the principal gods of the Cherokees. The

Cherokees considered the Sun to be female. The Cherokees called the Sun "the apportioned", referring to her dividing night and day and perhaps life and death as well. The Cherokee believed that sacred fire, like the Sun, was an old woman. The Cherokees addressed fire by the epithets "Ancient White and Ancient Red."

The circle and cross motif also symbolized sacred fire. The Cherokees believed that the Moon was the Sun's brother. When an eclipse of the Moon occurred, the Indians believed that it was being swallowed by a giant frog in the upper world. The Cherokees would all run out of their houses yelling and making noises to frighten away the frog. The Cherokees always succeeded in frightening frogs away, thereby saving the Moon from destruction. The Moon was addressed as "a grandparent;" thereby showing a relationship of respect and affection to ancestors.

Another important Cherokee deity was Thunder, or Kanati, the Red Man, who lived above the sky vault in the east. The Red Man's voice was heavy, rolling crashes of thunder; while the voices of his two sons; The Thunder Boys, also called the Little Red Men, were metallic sounding thunder. He sometimes killed white men with lightening.

Creatures in the Upper World were much larger than those in This World; however, the beings of the Upper World were not subject to all of the rules that limited ordinary people in their behavior. The Cherokees regarded the river as a deity, calling him The Long Man. The eagle was another heavenly representative used by the Cherokees as a deity.

The clan was the most important entity in the life of the Cherokee. A person belonged to his mother's clan; his only kinsmen were those who could be traced through his mother. The most important and powerful man in a Cherokee's life was his mother's brother. The maternal uncle was responsible for the discipline of his sister's child. The uncle was the one who taught the child to hunt and wage war. The woman owned the dwellings. An ousted husband simply went back to his clan until he remarried. His children remained with his wife.

Since kinship was matrilineal, Cherokee women probably decided the matter of adoption and often had the power to determine the fate of captives. The Beloved Woman, Nancy Ward, saved the life of Mrs. William Bean, who was about to be burned at the stake. The Cherokee extended the same privileges to those who married or were adopted into the tribe as those who were born into the tribe. Mary Hughes eventually married her husband's murderer and refused to leave the tribe even after she was ransomed. Twenty boys captured during the French and Indian War cried and refused to eat when they were returned to their families.

A Cherokee homestead

Clan membership was essential to one's existence as a human being within the Cherokee society. Since clans were divided into peace or war clans, a Cherokee's clan determined his political alignment and his role in society. Kinship governed social relationships indicating possible marriage partners, designating friends, and identifying enemies. The clan protected the rights of its members by promptly avenging any offense committed against a kinsman. The clan which adopted a captive became liable for his misdeeds and responsible for avenging wrongs done to him. Some captives were never adopted into a clan. These people, called the atsi nahsa'i, had no personal or legal protection. Their very existence depended on their master's good will.

The Cherokee tribe has many famous members who have contributed greatly to the welfare of its people; Sequoyah is one of these people. Sequoyah single-handedly created a written language for his people. His mother was Wah-teh, a Cherokee; his father was thought to be Nathaniel Guess, a white trader. Sequoyah's uncle was Doublehead, who lived in Lawrence County for some 12 years. Sequoyah, lame in one leg, became a fine silversmith and artist.

Sequoyah realized that the white man's "talking leaves" could provide a tremendous advantage. He drew a picture to represent each word, but there were so many that he realized this was impossible. He devised a symbol for each of the sounds of the Cherokee language. When he finished in 1821, he had eighty-five characters to symbolize every sound.

Sequoyah encountered many problems before he completed his project. He neglected his family responsibilities. Once, his angry wife burned two years of his work. Sequoyah and his young daughter, Ah-Yoka, went to a deserted cabin in the mountains and Sequoyah started working again. Since many Indians believed that Sequoyah's strange marks meant he was in league with the devil, they burned his cabin while he was away. Fortunately, Sequoyah remembered his symbols.

In 1821 when his work was completed, Sequoyah and his daughter demonstrated his symbols to the Cherokees. Within a few years, almost all the young and middle-age men in the Cherokee Nation could read and write the alphabet. The first Indian newspaper, The Cherokee Phoenix, was published. Bibles, pamphlets, and other materials were printed using Sequoyah's syllabary (Satz, 1979).

Sequoyah helped negotiate the Turkey Town Treaty of 1816 which gave up Lawrence, Morgan, and Franklin Counties. Shortly after the Treaty was approved, Sequoyah moved west to Arkansas. Sequoyah died in 1843 while looking for lost Cherokees in Mexico.

Creek Lifestyle

The homes, weapons, clothing and food of the Creek Indians were very similar to that of other Southeastern tribes because of geography and climate. Two major differences between the Creek and other Southeastern Tribes were the Creek form of government and the Creek Indian War of 1813-1814.

Menawa, Creek Warrior

Creek Indians brought many different tribes together to form a Creek Nation or a confederacy. By the year 1600, the Creek Nation had accepted the Alibamos, Koasatis, and Hitchitis. Later they accepted the Apalachees, Shawnees, Yuchis, Yamasees, Natchez, and many others.

Creek tribes were often named for their towns at one time, there were forty-five for more Creek towns with a population of 15,000 to 20,000 people.

These people spoke six different languages, had their own customs, and their own chiefs (Brown and Owens, 1984).

The name Creek was given to them by English traders who called the Indians living on the Ochese Creek in Georgia "Creek Indians". The Upper Creeks lived in about forty towns on the Coosa, Tallapoosa, and Alabama River. The Lower Creeks lived in about twenty towns on the Okmulgee, Flint, and Chattahoochee Rivers. Each division had a head chief called a micco. The micco ruled over the tribal council. The chief sat on a high platform which raised him above other men.

The capital of the nation was at Tukabachee, an Upper Creek town on the Tallapoosa near present day Montgomery. Both a head chief and a war chief represented the nation.

Creek towns were known as either white towns or red towns. White towns were peace town. People in the peace towns carried out ceremonies not related to war like the green corn ceremony and the ball games. The nation's principal chief was always from the white town. Red towns were war towns. War ceremonies were carried out in the red towns. The people in the red towns organized war parties, led raids, and took care of religious ceremonies related to war.

By 1812, the once powerful Creek Confederacy had fallen back, because of whites, to a few small towns along the inland rivers of Alabama. When the Revolutionary War was over the colonists declared Creek land public land. Land hungry whites rushed in to claim the Creek land. The upper Creeks resisted the white settlers believing the United States would protect their rights. The Lower Creeks did not resist because they saw no point in fighting the white settlers.

The Creek Indian War of 1813-1814 threw the Creek Nation into chaos. Scattered skirmished between the white settlers and the Creeks started the Creek Indian War. A party of Creeks returning from Pensacola on a trading mission was attacked by whites at Burnt Corn Creek (in present day Baldwin County, Alabama). Word of the attacked spread among the Indians and they prepared for war. The settlers went to Fort Mims for protection. On August 30, 1813, one-thousand warriors under William Weatherford (Red Eagle, 3/8 Creek) advanced on Fort Mims. Five hundred people in the fort were killed in one of the bloodiest massacres in American history. History fails to point out that over 700 of our Creek brothers lost their lives in this so called massacre. For two years, Andrew Jackson led Volunteer troops against the Creeks.

A reconstructed Creek camp

The Creek Indian War is sometimes called the Red Stick War. The warriors in all the towns voted their allegiance by throwing their sticks or tomahawks either to a white or a red side of the council fire. The Indians favoring war became the Red Sticks (Upper Creeks). The Indians against the war became the White Sticks (Lower Creeks). The Upper Creeks fought against Andrew Jackson and his Tennessee Volunteers while the Lower Creeks allied themselves with the whites.

The Battle of Horseshoe Bend was the decisive battle in the war. In March 1814, at Horseshoe Bend on the Tallapoosa River in Alabama, the Creeks prepared for a last desperate stand against Jackson and his army which included Creek and Cherokee Indians. In the horseshoe-shaped bend, about a thousand

Creeks under the command of Red Eagle and Chief Menawa gathered for battle. Women and children were sent down the river to safety. Canoes were hidden along the riverbanks for escape. A breastwork of logs was built to protect the land approach. Jackson had 2,000 foot soldiers, 700 cavalrymen, 600 Cherokee and some lower Creeks. At the end of the battle over 500 Creeks were killed and another 300 were shot trying to escape across the river.

William McIntosh, chief of the Lower Creeks, signed away all Creek land at the Treaty of Indian Springs in 1825. In 1828, the first Creek moved west to take up land promised them by the United States.

In 1836, General Winfield Scott with several thousand troops and a few Lower Creek chiefs set out to end the "Creek Rebellion". General Scott made prisoners of the Chiefs and leaders who protested the U.S. takeover of their land. In 1836, the Creek people were ordered out of Alabama. With some of their chiefs in chains, some 14,000 Creeks were forcibly moved to Oklahoma (Brown and Owens, 1984).

Chickasaw Lifestyle

The Chickasaws were smaller in number (never more than 5,000), yet claimed a larger region from northeast Mississippi into northwest Alabama and north into Tennessee, Kentucky and even Ohio; they were noted for the defense of their territory. The Chickasaw were probably related to the Choctaws. In the Choctaw language Chickasaw means, "They left as a tribe not a very great while ago" (Brown and Owens, 1984). The two tribes separated sometime before the arrival of the white man. They shared the same language and many of the same customs. The Chickasaw were noted for their physical characteristics. The Chickasaws were taller than their Choctaw cousins women 5' 10 to 6' tall (Brown and Owens, 1984). Chickasaw had light reddish skin and dark hair and eyes. Because of their dignity and nature, they were known as great warriors.

The Chickasaw gained a reputation of being warlike people. Before the white people came, Chickasaws had a different feeling about warfare. Chickasaws early in their history had little desire to conquer or do away with another tribe or acquire another tribe's land or possessions. Warfare was conducted with much ceremony and less killing than war in Europe at the same time (Brown and Owens, 1984). Chickasaw raids occurred in retaliation for raids made on the attackers.

The Chickasaws believed that the success of the raids depended on the prewar ceremonies. The great warrior or war chief supervised the three day preparation for the raid. The men ate nothing, but drank the black drink. The black drink was made from the leaves of a variety of holly (Hex Vomitoria). The black drink had a very high caffeine content that caused them to vomit and sweat. The drink was supposed to purify the Chickasaws for battle. Older men told stories of brave deeds to encourage the young warriors. They painted their bodies with war paint made from iron ore mixed with bear grease, berry stain, or ashes from the fire. A raiding party was made up of thirty or forty men. Each warrior carried a bow and arrow, a knife, and a war club spiked with fish teeth stuck through his belt. Their back pack held a blanket, a bag of parched corn, a wooden cup, and leather to repair moccasins (Brown and Owens, 1984). The Chickasaw had the reputation for being unconquered and unconquerable.

The Chickasaws sided with British and later with the Americans. According to many historians, it is the Chickasaw who received credit for the United States being an English-speaking nation (Wright, 1951). Small groups of Chickasaw were believed to have defeated much larger groups of French soldiers and Indian braves. The object of a Chickasaw raid was to surprise an enemy. As a surprise tactic, the group divided into smaller groups of three or four, traveling single file. The warriors stepped in each other's tracks so it would appear that there was only one person. They kept in touch by imitating animal sounds. Scouts were sent in four directions. The scout to the right imitated the call of an owl if he saw an enemy. The scout to the left imitated a wolf. The scout to the rear imitated a fox. The scout on the front imitated a bird.

Often Chickasaw attackers were satisfied with touching the victims with a special stick called coup. Touching was considered as brave an act as killing. Sometimes the war party took scalps. Indians did little scalping before the arrival of the white man. A scalping knife was a part of every pioneer's equipment. The European governments often offered bounties fur Indian Scalps.

Three days of celebration followed the return of a successful war party. The celebrations centered around the young men who had proved their bravery.

The warriors received war names and earned the right to wear a certain feather. Warriors were tattooed to record their brave deeds. Chickasaw warriors did not have to tend fires, light pipes, and serve the older men.

The Chickasaw marriage customs were similar to those of the other civilized tribes. The Chickasaw family was formed when a suitor selected a woman from another clan and followed a prescribed marriage ceremony (Gibson, 1971). The suitor would send the woman a gift with her acceptance meaning engagement. The marriage ceremony was the exchange of presents before witnesses. The man would select a "choice ear of corn and divide it in half before witnesses and give her one half and keep the other half" (Gibson, 1971). He would give her a deer's foot as an emblem of the readiness with which she ought to serve him, and in return she would give him some cakes of bread.

Polygamy (having more than one wife) was permitted among all Southeastern tribes. A man would choose wives who were sisters so he would not be required to establish a separate residence. If the wives were from different clans, he would have to establish separate residences and visit his women on a circuit. Chickasaw permitted a form of companioned marriage. Toopsa Tawa which means "make haste marriage" was a compassionate marriage (Gibson, 1971). The compassionate marriage did not require the usual ceremonies and duration of other marriages.

The Chickasaw widow was to remain single for four years unless her dead husband's sister arranged a marriage. Chickasaw widow tradition permitted both separation and divorce. Adultery was a serious offense; a guilty woman could be whipped, her hair shorn, and face disfigured. A man's only punishment was usually that issued by an irate husband or a wife's clan. Chickasaw practiced son-in-law and mother-in-law avoidance.

Children were primarily the responsibility of the mother. Chickasaw mothers followed the Choctaw practice on flattening the infant's forehead with a block of wood covered with buckskin or a bag of sand. The practice lasted into the late prehistoric period (Gibson, 1971). Male children were placed on panther skins to convey strength and cunning. Female children were placed on the skins of fawns or buffalo calves, because they were shy and timorous. The children were related to the mother's household or clan, not the father's. The girls were disciplined by the mother. The boys were disciplined by the oldest uncle of the mother's family. Women were responsible for the up-bringing of the girls, and the elders of the village took responsibility for the care instruction of the boys.

The Chickasaws' government was an extension of the clan system. The clans and towns were self-governing units of the tribe. Officials in the tribal government held their position because of clan status. The clan was governed by a council of elders and a Minko, a Chickasaw word meaning chief. The Minko was selected by the clan council. Each tribe had a head chief and other lesser chiefs.

Carolina Parakeets on Flint Creek. Drawing by Janice Barrett-Moore

The Chickasaw followed a prescribed religion incorporated their concept of a deity, creation, migration, and the ultimate or last things, such death, judgment, heaven, and hell (Gibson, 197). The deity concepts was centered around Ababinili, a composite force consisting of the four-Beloved Things, Above-Sun, Clouds Clear Sky, and He that Lives in the Clear Sky. This composite force made all men out of mother earth. They believed that creatures produced light, darkness, mountains and forests. Each town had a sacred fire which represented the sun. Guardian priests watched over this fire and dispensed coals for household fires. This practice allowed the sacred fire to be brought into each home.

The Chickasaws believed in existence after death. The steps in preparing the departed for the journey after death were an integral part of their religion. The grave was dug inside the dead person's house. The body was prepared for burial. The Chickasaws washed the corpse, anointed the head with oil, painted the face red, and dressed him in his best clothes. Personal belongings and a supply of corn were buried with him. The body was placed in the sitting position facing west.

The formal mourning period lasted twelve moons and involved extinguishing the fire in his house. The Chickasaws believed the ghosts of those slain in battle haunted the dwellings of the living until revenged, blood for blood. The Chickasaw observed ceremonies, taboos, and sacrifices as a religious exercise to win favor with the composite force and lesser deities. This was a common practice among other southeastern tribes.

James Logan Colbert and his three Chickasaw wives had sons who were important men in Chickasaw history. In 1769, three Colbert brothers led a war party against the Cherokees, who were trying to establish settlements on the lower Tennessee River. George and William Colbert fought with General St. Clair against the Northern Indians in 1792. In July 1794, George Washington called the brothers to the U.S. Capitol to thank them for their services to the United States.

George Colbert operated a ferry and lodging and eating house for travelers at Buzzard Roost which was near the spot where the Natchez Trace would cross the Tennessee River. George Colbert, who was head chief of the Chickasaw for twelve years, became the wealthiest man in the Chickasaw Nation. His name appears on all the important treaties between his tribe-and the U.S.

In 1786, George Colbert, Chief Piomingo, gave up five square miles on Tennessee River near present-day Muscle Shoals for a trading post. Most of the Colbert family went west with the tribe. Colbert County in Northwest Alabama-was the home of this remarkable Chickasaw family and bears their name today (Gibson, 1971.)

Chief Colbert's Ferry at the Natchez Trace on the Tennessee River.

Choctaw Lifestyle

Even though there are records of Choctaws living south of the area of the Warrior Mountains, the Choctaws influence and assistance in war against Creeks had an impact on our history.

It is believed that the Choctaws and Chickasaws came as one people into the south. The Choctaws moved into central and southern Mississippi and into southwest Alabama. Historians have always referred to the tribe as one of the most advanced, peaceful, and practical of all tribes. Prehistoric Choctaws flattened the foreheads of their children. This custom was picked up from the Siouan people. One method was to place the baby on a flat cradle board that was hinged so that it pressed the skull. Another method was to press the baby's head against the cradleboard with sandbags. It must be noted that skeletons with flattened skulls have been found in the Lawrence County portion of the Tennessee Valley near Big Nance Creek.

The most unusual custom of the Choctaws was the burial of their dead. The body was covered with skins and bark; and placed on a raised platform near the house. Food, drinks, clothing and personal possessions were placed with the body to aid it on its long journey into the next life. A dog was often killed and placed with the body to provided companionship on the journey; a fire close by provided light and warmth for the journey. The body stayed on the platform until it decomposed. During this time, the friends and family of the deceased came to mourn regularly. When the body had decomposed, "buzzard men" or bone pickers came and picked the remaining flesh from the bones. The bones were cleaned and placed in a box or basket and taken to the bone house. At special times, all the bones in the bone house were brought out for special mourning ceremonies.

A Choctaw woman

The Choctaws were small people, about five feet six inches in contrast to the Cherokee and Chickasaws who were closer to 6 feet tall. The Choctaws wore their hair long while other tribes in the southeast wore scalp locks.

Throughout history, the Choctaw people were farmers. Hunting took second place to farming. Choctaws grew corn, beans, squash, melons, and pumpkins in plots beside their homes. Corn was stored in cribs built of poles about eight feet off the ground. Their farming methods were so good they were able to sell their surplus to the Chickasaws. Stickball was the favorite game of the Choctaws. The stickball game was an important part of the green com ceremony. The game, often called the Little Brother of War, was a way to relieve tension and settle disputes between groups (Brown and Owens, 1984).

The Choctaws had a well-organized government with the Nation divided into three districts with separated chiefs. The Western Districts was called "Okla Falaya," meaning long time or long people. The Northeastern District was called the "Ahi Vpvt Okla" meaning, "potato eating people." The Southeastern District was formed by joining several districts together who called themselves the "Okla Hannabi" or "Six Towns" (Steffens and Chisholm, 1983).

The Choctaw religion was influenced by nature. The Choctaws believed that the Sun watched them with great blazing eyes and as long as it was on them everything was all right. If the sun's eye was not shining on them, they were doomed (Brown and Owens, 1984).

Warrior Mountains Indian Removal

For some 12,000 years prior to the early 1800's, all of the entire area throughout the Warrior Mountains was inhabited, controlled, and ruled by our aboriginal ancestors. Through early European explorations of DeSoto in 1540, other adventurous expeditions, military campaigns, and encroachments by early settlers, our native people were weakened by the ravages of diseases and wars that wiped out entire villages and towns. The tragic stage for the decimation of our Warrior Mountains Indian people was finally set after some 275 years of fighting diseases and wars brought about by the lust and greed of the European invaders.

The High Town or Ridge Path followed the east-west Continental Divide through the Warrior Mountains and was considered our Creek ancestors northern boundary. The northern drainage of the Warrior Mountains became the occupied home lands of the Chickasaws and Cherokees around the 1750's.

Long before their occupation, the Tennessee Valley was claimed as hunting territory for both tribes. The southern drainage of the Divide was occupied by our Creek ancestors when DeSoto marched his army through Alabama in 1540. It was the lands in the heart of the Warrior Mountains that Creek people had called home for hundreds of years.

Finally, our native people began to crumble from the European onslaught and pressure. The first native lands of the Warrior Mountains were threatened by the Cotton Gin Treaty of 1806. Later, the Treaty of Fort Jackson in 1814 took all our Creek homelands in the Warrior Mountains, south of the High Town Path. Within two years, the Turkey Town Treaty of September 16 and 18, 1816, had taken the last remnants of our aboriginal ancestors' native lands in the Warrior Mountains. The following years of forced removal decimated our native people who had lived for thousands of years in harmony with the land of the Warrior Mountains.

The Southeastern Indians became a conquered people. This was not done quickly, easily, or by a single method. The Indians were conquered militarily, but only in part, for they were able to withstand military onslaught. Through treaties which were legally and legislatively favoring the whites, our aboriginal lands were taken by the government. Many Indian people were removed from their homelands and forced to emigrate west of the Mississippi River. This removal represents one of the harshest, most opportunistic acts in American history. Details of removal for the four major Southeastern Indian Tribes can be found in the book "Indian Removal" by Grant Foreman.

Brief History of the Cherokee Decline

In 1763, the war, known as the French and Indian War, between the French and British ended with the British victorious in controlling most of the eastern North America. In addition to ending the war, a Proclamation Line of 1763 was established to protect the Indians west of the Appalachians and to halt encroachment on their lands. The Proclamation Line did not prevent settlers from invading Indian lands west of the line.

Eventually, the Cherokee were forced into making land cessions west of the Appalachians. In 1768, 1770, 1772, and 1773, treaties were made between the government and the Cherokee Indians. The Cherokee were pressured to give up land claims in South Carolina, Georgia, Virginia, West Virginia, Kentucky, and Tennessee. The Treaty of Sycamore Shoals, in 1775, took Cherokee lands through the middle of Kentucky and Tennessee.

Now, with the door to settlement opened, settlers poured into the area north of the Little Tennessee River to the heart of the once powerful Cherokee Nation. As the settlers moved in from the north and east, the Cherokees began moving south and west. By the 1750's, Cherokees were occupying eastern Alabama. By 1770, the Cherokees under Doublehead's leadership were firmly established in the area of the Warrior Mountains to the Muscle Shoals.

The Cherokee decline and loss of lands continued after the Revolutionary War partly because of their alliance with the British. The Middle, Valley, and Overhill Towns of the Cherokee were practically destroyed by military movements lead against the Cherokees by men such as Colonel William Christian and Colonel John Sevier. Eventually in 1780, the armies of John Sevier and Arthur Campbell destroyed the Overhill Towns including the Cherokee Capitol of Chota. By this time, a thriving population of Cherokee was occupying the lower Tennessee Valley.

Many of the Cherokee moved south under the leadership of Dragging Canoe, son of Oconostota. The Cherokees under Dragging Canoe settled from Chattanooga to the south and west in five villages referred to as the "Five Lower Towns on the Tennessee" (Running Water, Nickajack, Long Island Village, Crow Town, and Lookout Mountain Town).

Cherokee Chief Doublehead migrated farther southwest along the Tennessee River into north Alabama; historical evidence indicates Doublehead settled for some 30 years at the head of Elk River Shoals at Doublehead's Town. Doublehead helped establish the following villages along the Tennessee River in Lawrence County: Monee Town at the mouth of Fox's Creek, Doublehead's Town at Brown's Ferry between Fox and Mallard Creeks; Melton's Bluff between Mallard and Spring Creeks; Gourd's Settlement at Courtland on Big Nance Creek; and, Shoal Town between the creeks called Big Nance, Blue Water, and Town Creek just west of present day Wheeler Dam.

In east Tennessee, by the 1780's, the Cherokee were a defeated people trying to survive in a country controlled by a newly established government of the United States. Devastated by war, disease, and land hungry American settlers, their day's east of the Mississippi River were numbered.

By the beginning of the 1800's, the once flourishing towns along the Little Tennessee River were practically abandoned by the Cherokee people. By 1816 even the lands along the Great Mussel Shoals were taken by the Turkey Town Treaty. Then in 1830 Indian Removal Act spelled doom for many Cherokee. Two years after the Treaty of New Echota in 1836, the Army of Winfield Scott attempted to remove all the Cherokee remaining east of the Mississippi. The remnants of the Cherokee and mixed bloods that remained in the east were a scattered and defeated people living in a state of denial of their aboriginal beginnings, but in their hearts holding to their beliefs.

Doublehead and Removal

From the 1770's, Chief Doublehead and the Chickamauga inhabited and controlled the area of the Warrior Mountains and north to the present day Tennessee State Line. About 1770, Doublehead settled and lived in Lawrence County at Doublehead's Town which was at the head of Muscle Shoals near

Brown's Ferry. The following text tells of Doublehead's home and is found on page 62 of Volume V, "The Journal of Muscle Shoals History," and written in a speech by William B. Wood published in 1876 is the following:

"As early as 1802, a party set out from North Carolina, who, with great difficulty, ascended the Blue Ridge, with their wagons, and descended through its gorges, into the valley of the Tennessee. Constructing flat boats at Knoxville, they floated down the Tennessee River, to the head of Muscle Shoals, where they disembarked at the house of Doublehead, a Cherokee Chief. This party, however did not remain in this valley, the lands belonging to the Indians, their title having not yet been extinguished."

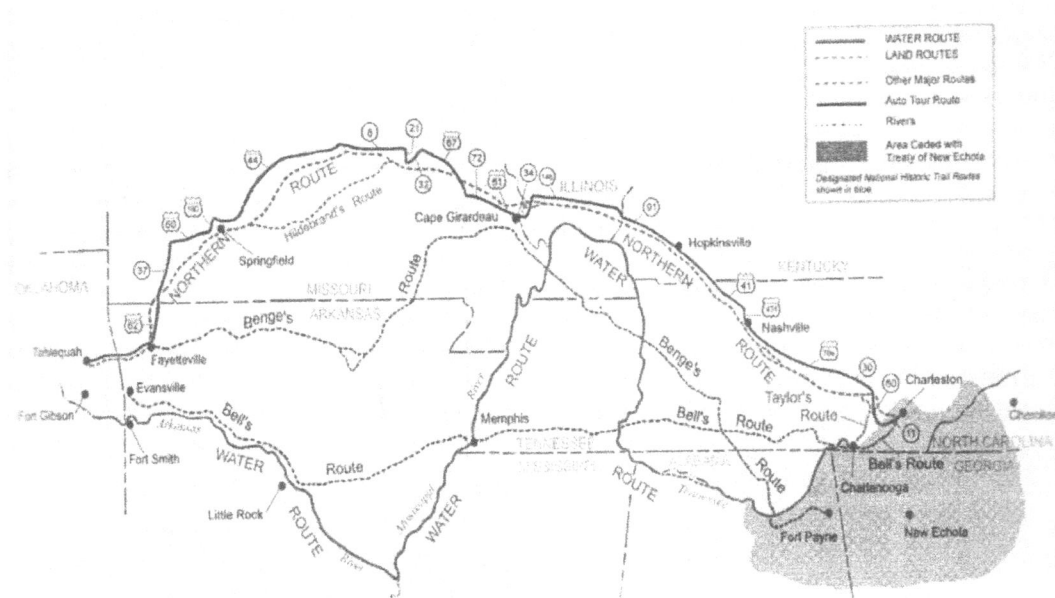

Sometime around the early 1800's, Doublehead moved down river to join his nephew Tahlontuskee at Shoal Town-the Blue Water/Town Creek Village. According to William L. McDonald's "The Lore of Chief Doublehead and His Home at Muscle Shoals" found in Volume IX of the Journal of Muscle Shoals History on page 103 is the following:

"Yet, Doublehead was without influence or position. That is, until about the year 1790, when he established his first town on the Tennessee River at the head of the Muscle Shoals. An early map of the Cherokee Country shows this village at a site near the south bank of Brown's Ferry below Athens. He later moved it to the north bank of the river near the mouth of Blue Water Creek, in Lauderdale County, Alabama."

According to historical information, Doublehead lived at Doublehead's Town from 1770 until 1802 at the head of Muscle Shoals on the south bank of the Tennessee River in present day Lawrence County. The Cherokee village is also shown on a 1779-1796 map of the proposed "State of Franklin." Doublehead's Town was located between Mallard Creek and Fox's Creek. Doublehead lived at his town prior to moving to his Blue Water home in present day Lauderdale County. Doublehead's old two story log home and tavern was destroyed during the four laning of Highway 72 between Athens and Florence.

Tahlontuskee Benge, the nephew of Doublehead, had his settlement at Shoal Town near the mouths of Town Creek in Lawrence County and Blue Water Creek in Lauderdale County on the banks of the Hogohegee (Tennessee) River, known as the "River of the Cherokees." The village actually lay on both sides of the river about six miles from the eastern upstream end of the Big Mussel Shoals.

Actually at this point, the Blue Water Ferry crossed the river from the eastern point of Blue Water Creek to the area halfway between Town Creek and Big Nance Creek in present day Lawrence County. According to Nina Leftwich's book *Two Hundred Years at Muscle Shoals*, the Cherokees had a large settlement at the mouth of Town Creek, which extended a mile along the river and far up the creek.

Doublehead was the feared Chickamauga war chief of the lower Tennessee River Cherokees. His nephew, Tahlonteskee, was probably the peace chief, since each Cherokee village had both a war chief and a peace chief. Shoal Town at the mouths of Blue Water, Town Creek, and Big Nance Creeks was the final Alabama home of both men. Doublehead is supposedly buried on the north side of present-day highway 72 just east of Blue Water Creek in Lauderdale County, Alabama.

1809 Cherokee Removal

In 1806, Cherokee Chief Doublehead, his great nephew Tahlonteskee, and other Cherokees signed the Cotton Gin Treaty which gave up Cherokee claims to land north of the Tennessee River except for Doublehead's Reserve. The reserve lay between Elk River (Chuwalee) and Cypress Creek (TeKeetanoeh) in present day Lauderdale County.

The signing of the Cotton Gin Treaty brought the wrath of other Cherokee leaders upon the individuals who signed the treaty giving up Cherokee Lands. Major Ridge, a powerful Cherokee leader, made known that Doublehead and others would pay with their lives for relinquishing Cherokee lands. At a meeting of Cherokee headmen in Tennessee, Doublehead paid with his life at the hand of Ridge, Alex Saunders, John Rogers, and their accomplices. Alex Saunders and John Rogers had ties to Lawrence County and probably profited from the assassination of Doublehead.

After the assassination of Chief Doublehead by his own people, due to the circumstances of the Cotton Gin Treaty of 1806, several Cherokees living in the Lawrence County area and related to Doublehead moved west to avoid the same fate. The following is from "The Cherokees" by Grace Steele Woodard published in 1963 and found on page 131:

"However, in 1808, the Compact 1802 was not needed to effect the removal of some 1,130 Chickamaugans to lands west of the Mississippi (today Dardanelle, Arkansas, in Pope County). Jefferson had merely to suggest to Tahlonteskee and other Chickamaugans that if they did not care to remain in the same country with their enemy countrymen, they could remove to Dardanelle Rock. Thus, in the spring of 1808, Tahlontuskee fearing assassination notified President Jefferson that his people were ready to migrate. Following their migration, Tahlonteskee's band of Cherokees called themselves "Cherokees West" or "Old Settlers."

Since Tahlonteskee signed the 1806 Cotton Gin Treaty, he feared the same punishment that Doublehead received for giving up land north of the Tennessee River; therefore, he and his Cherokee followers agreed to move from Shoal Town at the Blue Water/Town Creek Village on the Big Muscle Shoals of the Tennessee

River to the west during the summer of 1809. It is believed by some that Sequoyah, George Guess, went west after the 1816 Turkey Town Treaty in search of his half brother, Tahlonteskee.

1816 Cherokee Removal

Even though some Cherokees in the Warrior Mountains area left with Tahlonteskee's group in 1809, many Cherokee people still lived in the Tennessee Valley from the river to the High Town Path in southern Lawrence County. Within the great valley of the Tennessee, cotton became the agricultural "king" for making money. With the new government cotton gin at Melton's Bluff and black slaves for farm labor, both the Chickasaws and Cherokees, who shared ownership of the river valley, became wealthy; however, the government and settlers wanted the cotton wealth of the Tennessee Valley which was controlled by the Indians.

In 1816, with several more years of pressure, the Chickasaws and Cherokees finally relinquished their claim to the remainder of Warrior Mountains. Therefore, due to the circumstances of the Turkey Town Treaty of September 16 and 18, 1816, another contingent of Chickasaws and Cherokees moved west, from the land of the Warrior Mountains in Lawrence County, Alabama. The first documented removal from Melton's Bluff in Lawrence County is found in the following excerpt given in the 1969 printing of *Letters from Alabama 1817-1822* by Anne Royall on pages 134 and 135 with the Letter XXIV dated January 14, 1818:

"Melton's Bluff is a town, and takes its name person by the name of John Melton, a white ceased two years since, at an advanced age ...You recollect Rhea whom I have mentioned: he married one of Melton's daughters-a most amiable woman, and very lame. When the Cherokee Indians abandoned this territory last fall, some of them went up the river to the Cherokee nation, there to remain till boats were provided for their removal to the west, by the government; others went directly down the river to Arkansas-of whom Rhea's wife was one.

The order for their departure was sudden and unexpected. Rhea, at that time was absent from home, but returned on the same day and learning what had happened, was almost frantic jumped into a canoe, and soon overtook the boats.

He flew to his wife, and clasped her in his arms. Neither spoke a word, but both wept bitterly. In a few moments-be resumed his canoe and returned to the Bluff, and she went on. They had no children. Whether Rhea was prohibited by the treaty from accompanying his wife, or whether he was under a prior engagement, none here are able to inform me-but certain it is, he is now married to a white woman."

Rhea had moved to Melton's Bluff about 1803 and had married one of John Melton's half-blood Cherokee daughters. According to Royall, he had guided as many as four boats at a time, ten dollars each, through the Elk River Shoals, Big Mussel Shoals, and Little Mussel Shoals for some 15 years. Also, at this time, James Melton, Rhea's half-blood Cherokee brother-in-law, was a river boat guide that piloted boats through the Shoals for Malcolm Gilchrist, one of the early settlers of the Courtland area.

Shortly after the Turkey Town Treaty was signed, several Cherokees left Melton's Bluff in Lawrence County for: lands in the west during the fall of 1816. In addition, Andrew Jackson did not wait until the dust of the 1816 removal had settled to begin staking his claims to Indian lands and property in Lawrence County.

Jackson Exploits Removal

Just after the Turkey Town Treaty of 1816, Melton's Bluff came under the ownership of General Andrew Jackson. David Melton was the half-blood Cherokee son of Irishman John Melton. According to Anne Royall's letter on January 14, 1818, John Melton died two years prior; according to his wife Ocuma, John died on June 7, 1815. After the death of John Melton, Andrew Jackson pressured Melton's son into selling the plantation. The following is an excerpt from *Melton's Bluff* by William L. McDonald:

"General Andrew Jackson in partnership with his wife's nephew, Colonel John Hutchings, purchased Melton's Bluff from a David Melton in 1816. It is believed that David was a son of the old pirate, John Melton. This deed, signed **November 22, 1816,** *described the property as follows:*

"I David Melton of the Cherokee Nation do by these presents bargain and sell ... unto General Andrew Jackson and Captain John Hutchings all my right title and interest to the tract of land where I now live, and agree to give them possession of all the improvements laying north and east of the spring, including said spring, on said tract where I live and adjoining where I live, and the houses and ... land southeast of the spring. Possession to be given of as many Negro houses as will house the Negroes of the said Andrew and the said John ... and possession of the other houses on or before the first day of February... For which I acknowledge to have received the consideration of sixty dollars in cash and in full of the above sale."

Just prior to the fall removal in 1816, Melton's family along with other Cherokees went to the west or Cherokee lands to the east; Andrew Jackson acquired not only the land that belonged to the Melton family, but also about sixty slaves and other possessions. The Indian fighter had now gone full circle by enlisting Cherokees to fight the Creeks, then beating the Cherokees out of their land and possessions; but, Jackson had much worse in store with the Indian Removal Act of 1830.

1818 Cherokee Removal

After Jackson had acquired Melton's Bluff which he named Marathon, another group Cherokee's was facing removal. On January 20, 1818, while at Melton's Bluff, Anne Royall observed some 300 Cherokees camped just two miles east of the Bluff in Lawrence County. These Cherokees were in the process of moving west of the Mississippi River. The following writing was found in Letter XXX dated January 20, 1818 and on pages 154 and 155 of the book *Letters from Alabama 1817-1822*:

"Hearing eleven boats had arrived about two miles from hence, and had halted up the river; we set off, as I said before, in a little canoe, to see the Indians, which are on their way to their destination beyond the Mississippi. Government, agreeably to their contract, having completed the boats, the news of the arrival of the Indians had been received with much interest; but being unable to proceed by water, we quit the canoe, and proceeded by land in our wet shoes and hose.

We *arrived at the Indian camps about eleven o'clock. There were several encampments at the distance of three hundred yards from each other, containing three hundred Indians. The camps were nothing, but* some *forks of wood driven into the ground, and a stick lay across them, on which hung a pot in which they* were *boiling meat; I took it to* be *venison. Around* these *fires were seated,* some *on the ground, some on logs, and some on chairs, females of all ages; and all employed, except the old women. There were some very old gray-haired women, and several children at each camp. The children were very pretty; but the grown females were not."*

Above: Andrew Jackson tried to annihilate the Creek Confederacy.

The group of Cherokees observed by Royall was probably waiting for a rise in the river in order to pass through the Elk River Shoals safely. Keelboats and flatboats waited at the head of Brown's Island until the water conditions permitted safe passage. At Brown's Island, the river channel divided as it passed around either side. Before the channels rejoined on the island's downstream end, rapids on both sides of the island created dangerous situations for boats. At the upstream end of Brown's Island was Brown's Ferry which Ms. Royall said was visible eight miles upstream from Melton's Bluff. It was near Brown's Ferry at the head of the shoals where Doublehead had lived until about 1802.

Water Route through Warrior Mountains

By 1830, Andrew Jackson had successfully gotten the Indian Removal Act passed by Congress. The intent of the act was to remove all Indian people from the Eastern United States to areas west of the Mississippi River. Many Indian removals had already been completed but Jackson wanted all native people removed from the East. One of the major routes of Cherokee removal was down the Tennessee River through Muscle Shoals toward the west.

During 1831, work began on the construction of a canal around Big Mussel Shoals to aid in the navigation of the Tennessee River. The government had released 400,000 acres to be sold for funds to complete the canal. The following if found in Nina Leftwich's book *Two Hundred Years at Muscle Shoals*, *"A land office was established at Courtland in 1829 to dispose of the lands given to the state for the purpose of building the canal around the Shoals. Dr. Jack Shackleford was made receiver for the Courtland office and the lands were soon disposed of and the office was closed."*

Some $644,000.00 was used in the construction which was completed in 1836; however, during low water, Elk River Shoals prevented downstream traffic and Little Muscle Shoals prevented upstream traffic. The old canal was eventually abandoned in 1838 and soon filled with sediment.

In addition to the contingents of Cherokees who lived in and were removed west from Lawrence County, other groups of Cherokee were removed west through the Elk River Shoals, Big Mussel Shoals, and Little Mussel Shoals of the Tennessee River, while the canal was being built. During high-water seasons, keel boats and flatboats could pass over the hazards of the Shoals if extreme caution was observed.

1832-1834 Cherokee Removal by Water

During the first voluntary removals, many Cherokees traveled through the rapids of Elk River Shoals, Big Mussel Shoals, and Little Mussel Shoals to areas west of the Mississippi. The well-known water removals of Cherokees down the Tennessee through the Muscle Shoals included the Currey removal contingent of Cherokees who passed by Melton's Bluff and through the Muscle Shoals on flatboats in 1832. The following is from *Indian Removal* by Grant Foreman:

Currey was ready by April 1832 to depart with the little band collected by him. The Cherokees he said "dread the length of time necessarily consumed in passing on board of flat-bottomed boats to the mouth of White River, as they are not accustomed to long voyages, would be liable to contract disease". Instead of the thousand emigrants promised him, he had but 380 persons, 108 blacks, forty whites, and the remainder mixed, with a few full-bloods. Twenty-one were from Tennessee and the remainder from Georgia.

They left the Cherokee agency at Calhoun on April 10 in nine flatboats, and passing down the Tennessee river through the rapids at Muscle Shoals, arrived a week later at Waterloo. They were transferred to the steamboat Thomas Yeatman which departed about the twentieth and passed out of the mouth of the Tennessee River three days later. They proceeded down the Ohio and Mississippi and up the Arkansas river, reaching Little Rock on the thirtieth, part of them were disembarked at the Cherokee Agency just above Fort Smith, on the left bank of the Arkansas River, and the remainder were taken farther up to the mouth of the Illinois."

Again in 1834, Benjamin F. Currey's contingent of Cherokees passed through the Muscle Shoals. Curry, who was superintendent of removal, utilized Lieutenant Joseph W. Harris of New Hampshire and West Point, graduate of the class of 1825, to conduct the Cherokee emigrants to their western home. The flatboats were set for departure on March 13, 1834. The following by Foreman's Indian Removal gives the detail:

Waiting for dilatory arrivals two weeks after the time set for departure, on March 13, 1834, the boats dropped down to the landing and the next afternoon when the John Cox and Sliger had taken on board seventy-two emigrants they cast off. *This party was in charge of Harris's assistant, a white man named John Miller who was married to a Cherokee woman; he was under orders to collect the stragglers and those living along the banks of the Hiwassee and Tennessee Rivers who were ready to depart and would be awaiting the boats; and then to wait at Muscle Shoals for the remainder of the party.*

Harris delayed the departure of the main body of emigrants until the arrival of a company of seventy mountain Indians known- as the Valley Town, who brought their belongings in three heavy six-horse wagons...

Doctor Edington of Calhoun accompanied the emigrants as far as Tuscumbia where he would be relieved by another. After ten days rations had been issued, the next day at eleven o 'clock the Blue Buck with 125 emigrants on board cast off an hour later "after some trouble in which persuasion, threats and force were alternately resorted to, the remainder of the party were embarked and

the Rainbow, the Squeezer and the Moll Thompson unmoored and dropped into the current.

At midnight the party overtook the Blue Buck moored snugly to the bank with all on board asleep. Her skipper was ordered to cast off and an hour later the boats passed out of the Hiwassee River into the Tennessee. At eight o'clock, twenty-five miles below, Harris overtook Miller's contingent at Brown's Ferry and by noon had joined the remainder of the fleet. Before night the boats successfully negotiated the shoals and rapids in the Tennessee River known as the "Suck," the "Boiling Pot," the "Frying Pan," and the "Skillet." After safely passing through the Muscle Shoals, they arrived at Waterloo, Alabama, on the nineteenth, having made 267 miles in six days of water travel. The voyage had been uneventful thus far, though considerable trouble had been caused by the introduction of whisky among the Indians whenever stops were made near white settlements, and numerous cases of measles had developed in the party.

It should be noted that both of the parties safely passed through the Muscle Shoals during March and April. During the spring of the year, water levels on the Tennessee were high enough to provide for uneventful passage of the dangerous Muscle Shoals. Future removal contingents were transported around the shoals probably because of the extreme danger of destroying boats and losing lives.

Railroad Route Through north Alabama

The first railroad west of the Alleghenies was built to carry goods and products around the Muscle Shoals. The railroad had stops at Hillsboro, Courtland, and Town Creek in Lawrence County to take on materials, water, and fuel. The following is a description of the rail line through Lawrence County as given on page 252 in the book *The Tennessee* by Donald Davidson in 1946.

"They built a railroad. It was a "dinky" railroad, by modern standard, but it was a railroad-the first one west of the Appalachians. In 1832, they ran a line over the short distance between Tuscumbia and the river. In 1834, they carried it east to Decatur, a distance of forty miles. This, the Tuscumbia, Courtland, and Decatur Railroad, was a very primitive affair, built of "string pieces of wood scantlings on which flat bars of iron, a half an inch by two and a

*half inches, were laid." But it served a great need, since it provided an easy
portage around Muscle Shoals, and it predicted more railroads and better
railroads to come."*

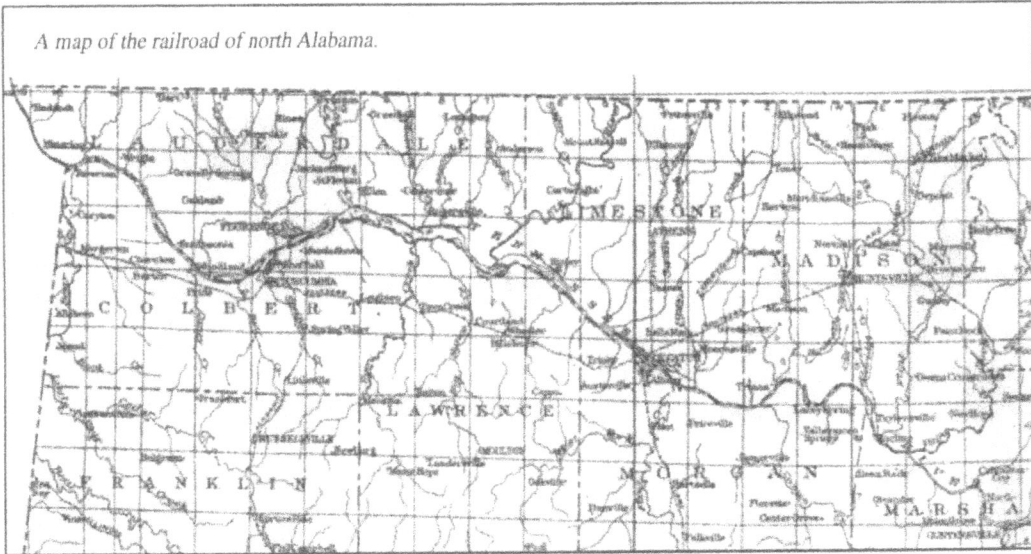

A map of the railroad of north Alabama.

Since the rails were so thin, they had a tendency to roll up on the end. The
turned up ends were called snake heads. A crew aboard the train would jump out
and hammer down the snake heads.

The great mussel shoals was a barrier to transportation and was the major
reason for constructing a rail line to Decatur from Tuscumbia. Even though the
primary purpose was for the transport of goods around the Muscle Shoals, the
railroad became a mechanism for Cherokee Removal during the forced removal
of 1837 and 1838.

1837-1838 Cherokee Removal by Railroad

After completion of the railroad, most of the Cherokee contingents
removed west were transported by the railroad from Decatur to Tuscumbia.
These Cherokees passed through Hillsboro, Courtland, and Town Creek in

Lawrence County on their way to the Tuscumbia Landing. At the landing, they would board boats for removal westward.

The following excerpt from page 224 and 225 of *Indian Removal* describes a March 3, 1837, Cherokee contingent moved by railroad through present-day Morgan, Lawrence, and Colbert Counties:

"The boats reached Gunter's Landing on the *sixth and were tied up to the island to prevent* the *Indians from going ashore and getting drunk... The steamer Knoxville was waiting for them here, and when the eleven flatboats were made fast to her, the flotilla set off at nine o'clock on the seventh...*

On their arrival at <u>*Decatur*</u>*, the Indians were placed on board open cars and compelled to sit in the cold from three-o'clock: until dark awaiting the engine that did not arrive. The bewildered Indians who had never before seen a railroad train were left to find a place to sleep; "The train of cars from the west was momentarily expected, and the Indians were afraid to lie down for fear of being run over. No lights were furnished them, and they were grouping in the dark, in a pitiful manner;" but their humane physician succeeded in having a warehouse opened for them in which they made their beds on the floor for the night. In the morning the emigrants were again placed on the cars that delivered them in Tuscumbia by night. Here they camped awaiting the arrival of the boats that were to take them down the river. While in camp it rained hard and long, the weather was cold and windy, and the Indians were wet, cold, and miserable.*

About ten o'clock on the thirteenth the steamboat Newark and two keel-boats arrived and "moored to the landing near which the Indians encamped; immediately the whole posse of them were in motion bringing their effects to the boats...."

It appears that the rail trip from Decatur to Tuscumbia took all day; therefore, the train probably stopped at each station and had several snake heads to nail down.

Again another excerpt from pages 292 and 293 describe the train route on June 8, 1838:

"The boats succeeded without incident in passing through the remainder of the rapids and into smooth water by noon the next day. They ran all that day and night; passed Gunter's Landing at nine o'clock, stopped once "to wood" and at night landed six miles above Decatur, "and such of the people as choose have gone ashore to sleep and cook." Starting early on the morning of the ninth they reached Decatur at six o'clock to take the train to Tuscumbia but were compelled to remain until the next day. Then "the Indians and their baggage were transferred from the boats to the Rail Road car. About 32 cars were necessary to transport the Party, and no Locomotive Engines."

"As the Indians were much crowded on the train the twenty-three soldiers were discharged. The first detachment reached Tuscumbia at three o'clock and boarded the steamboat Smelter which "immediately set off for Waterloo at the foot of the rapids without waiting for the 2nd train of cars with the remainder of the party." When the second party reached Tuscumbia they went into camp awhile awaiting transportation by water. As the guard had been discharged, whisky was introduced among them, much drunkenness resulting, and over one hundred of the emigrants escaped. The remainder was carried by water aboard a keel boat and a small steamer about thirty miles to Waterloo."

A third railroad contingent of removal Cherokees to be transported through Lawrence County around the Muscle Shoals occurred on June 21, 1838, as given on pages 294 and 295 of *Indian Removal*.

"On June 13 the second party of 875 captive Cherokee Indians departed from Chattanooga in charge of Lieut. R. H. K. Whiteley, with five assistant conductors, two physicians, three interpreters, and a hospital attendant. After the preceding day had been spent in organizing the party and reuniting separated families as far as possible, they were placed on six flatboats and dropped down the Tennessee river to Brown's Ferry where more prisoners joined them. For two days they remained there while clothing was purchased and offered to the Indians who refused to receive it "neither would they be mustered, as all attempts to obtain their names were without success."

When they left there the flotilla was increased to eight flatboats; tied together in pairs these safely negotiated the dangerous rapids and arrived at Kelly's Ferry in the evening. On the morning of the eighteenth with four flatboats

114

moored on each side, the steamboat George Guess continued the descent of the river. ...

On the twentieth they arrived at Decatur and the next morning departed on two trains, arriving at the boat landing below Tuscumbia in the evening. One old woman died at Decatur and a man was killed by the cars when he attempted to rescue his hat. Before reaching Decatur twenty-five Indians had escaped from the party. The emigrants were required to remain at Tuscumbia several days before boats could be secured to carry them over Colbert Shoals, and during their stay two children died. They passed the shoals on the twenty-eighth and encamped opposite Waterloo, Alabama, while awaiting the arrival of the steamboat Smelter. During the stay here, three children died, there was one birth, and 118 Indians escaped."

Even though most of the Cherokees had been forced from the area of the Warrior Mountains by 1817, many had to pass through their former homelands after Jackson negotiated the Indian Removal Act of 1830. Since many Cherokees of mixed ancestry had already hid out in the Warrior Mountains area by the 1830's, escapees of the emigrating Cherokees found refuge with friends and relatives located in the Lawrence County area.

Several events preceded the Cherokee Removal. On December 20, 1828, the Georgia legislature passed an act which declared that in any controversy arising between white people and Indians, the latter should be disqualified as witnesses. The Georgia law gave the whites absolute dominance over the Indians; leaders removed themselves and their families to Red Clay, Tennessee where tribal council meetings could be held.

The Indian Removal Act of May 28, 1830, provided for the consolidation of Indian lands. The Treaty of New Echota was signed by General William Caroll and John Schermerhorn representing the U.S. government on December 29, 1835, at New Echota, Georgia. Signing for the Cherokee were Major Ridge, James Tau - yeske, Archilla Smith, Andrew Rogers, John Gunter, John A. Bell, Charles Foreman, William Rogers, George Adair, Elais Boudinot, James Starr, and Jessie Half-breed (Previous Cherokee law dictated that it was illegal for anyone to sign away Cherokee land rights). The Treaty provided for the enrollment of the Cherokee for removal and for the appraisal of their property. The first party to be conducted westward by the government under the terms' of the New Echota Treaty consisted of 466 Cherokees, half of whom were children. This group assembled at Ross Landing (near the present-day city of Chattanooga, Tennessee) on March 1, 1837, to begin their journey. The group embarked in a fleet of eleven flatboats divided into three groups. On March 6, 1837, the boats reached Gunter's Landing and the next morning the flatboats were tied to the steamer Knoxville in order to proceed down the Tennessee River. Upon arriving in Decatur, the Indians were placed in railroad cars and delivered to Tuscumbia. From Tuscumbia, the group traveled on keel boats which were attached to the steamboat Newark; they were then taken to Little Rock and from there to Fort Coffee.

The second emigrating party set out from the Cherokee Agency at Calhoun, Tennessee on October 14, 1837, traveling overland through Kentucky, Illinois, and Missouri. The group was comprised of 357 Cherokees. Because of deprivation and hardship, fifteen deaths occurred on the march.

Forced Indian removal began in May of 1838. General Winfield Scott distributed his troops throughout the Cherokee country where stockade forts were erected for gathering in and holding the Indians preparatory to removal. Squads of troops were sent out from the forts to search for and detain any Indians hidden away in the caves and mountains.

Seventeen thousand Cherokees were collected into various stockades. Cherokees numbering around 5,000 were moved to Ross Landing and Gunter's Landing and were transported to the west bank of the Mississippi River, where the journey continued by land. The next twenty-eight hundred Cherokees were divided into three detachments, the first of which left Ross Landing on June 6, 1838. This group traversed a series of dangerous rapids called the Suck, the Boiling-pot, the Skillet, and the Frying pan on the Tennessee River. They traveled to Gunter's Landing and Decatur by boat and from there by train to Tuscumbia. Because there was so little room on the train, guards were dismissed and many escaped. Many of these Indian people remained in the area between Decatur and Tuscumbia, hid in the forest regions, and later married white persons or were able to identify them with white ancestry. From Tuscumbia, the remaining captives traveled by water to Waterloo, Paducah, Memphis and on to Little Rock and Fort Coffee. Many more expeditions were needed to move the

Cherokees to their new western homes. In October 1838, about 13,000 Cherokees began a long over land journey to the West, which ended in the spring of 1839. This particular march was noted in history as the "Trail of Tears." It is asserted that over 4,000 Cherokees died as a direct result of the removal. Many Cherokee mixed-bloods and their descendants avoided removal and remained in the Warrior Mountains of Lawrence County, Alabama.

Creek Indian Removal

During the days leading up to the Creek removal, our Creek Indian people became the most brutally treated inhabitants to be forced from the beloved Warrior Mountains. In Lynn Hastie Thompson's book *William Weatherford-His Country and His People* printed in 1991 and found on pages 429 and 430 is the following:

"Davy Crockett watched as about fifty Warriors ran into one hut... They then rushed the hut and set tire to it, burning alive the fifty warriors who had taken refuge inside ... A young boy about twelve ran from one of the burning houses and was shot down after only a few feet. The bullets had not killed him but had broken his arm and thigh, making him unable to move. Heat from the burning house began to cook his skin. Crockett saw the grease stewing out of him, but still not a murmur came from his mouth. Crockett knew that an Indian would sooner die than cry in pain or ask for quarter, but never had he witnessed so young a child withstanding such inhuman pain without crying out... the Creeks had met death and all its horrors without shrinking or complaining ... In the massacre, not only warriors, but also women and children were killed ... In the days that followed the battle as Davy Crockett boasted of the slaughter; "we shot them down like dogs... "

Many terrible and brutal acts stand as a reminder of the horror and pain our Creek people felt as they were being annihilated in their homes and villages. Even Davy Crockett, who stands as a hero to many, could have shown mercy. How could a hero watch a child die a slow death of horror regardless of the color of his skin; however, Crockett was serving under one of the most merciless military leaders to ever serve as President of the United States, Andrew Jackson. After Jackson's Army defeated the Creek people at The Horseshoe Bend, our native home-lands in the Warrior Mountains were taken by the Treaty of Fort Jackson in 1814.

Many Creeks that survived were of mixed ancestry and sought freedom as European descent claiming Black Dutch and Black Irish. Many sought isolation within the Warrior Mountains and slowly became assimilated into the general population. Many others sought the protection of their mixed relatives, or settler friends. For many, removal became the only answer.

Earlier, Jackson's army of East Tennessee Volunteers crossed the Hogohegee (Tennessee) River at Melton's Bluff in November 1813, and October 1814, during the Creek Indian War. Davy Crockett, the famous frontiersman, and third sergeant in Captain Cowan's Company, traveled with the army along Black Warriors' Path through the Oakville Park and Lawrence County to destroy Black Warrior Town. Later, along the same path used by Crockett and Jackson's army to defeat the Creeks, our noble Indian people traveled along the same route through Lawrence County in the removal to the west.

Fort Mitchell marked the southern-most point of the Mitchell Trace (Black Warriors Path) that passed through the Oakville Indian Mounds Park. The fort played a vital role in the final days of the Creek Indian removal during the 1830's. By 1835, many of our Creek people had been removed west or were in the process of being removed.

The passage of a detachment of our Creek people through the Warrior Mountains and Oakville Indian Mounds Park along the Mitchell Trace (Black Warriors' Path) was on December 19, 1835. The following text is from the book *Indian Removal* by Grant Foreman:

"Opothleyaholo promised that he and his people would be ready to remove the next April. Benjamin Marshall, a half-breed Creek, a member of the emigrating company that had contract for the removal of the Creeks, was anxious to take his family and slaves to the West that autumn. He was influential member of the tribe and largely through his efforts an emigrant party of 511 was organized on the Tallapoosa River near Wetumpka December 6, 1835. The party was made up of members from Fish Pond, Kealedji, Hilibi, and Asilanabi towns. They were accompanied by Marshall who had with him his family of eight and his

nineteen slaves. The party was conducted by Lieut. Edward Deas of the army detailed to see that the conditions of the contract for caring the Indians were observed by the contractors, represented by Doctor Ingersoll.

Ledagie, a Creek who visited Washington D.C. to protest Indian removal.

The agent attempted to enroll the Indians of his party in Tallapoosa County, but he "found it impossible to get a correct roll in the Nation in the *vicinity of so many grog shops," and he was obliged to take them across the Coosa River before he could count them. Traveling about twelve miles each day, they passed through Montavallo, and forded the Cawhawba river on the eleventh; passed Elyton, crossed two forks of the Black Warrior River, **the west fork of Flint creek, Moulton on the nineteenth**, and arrived at Tuscumbia the twenty-first. Hearing discouraging reports about the condition of the roads, Deas decided to take the Indians here by boat. Sending their horses in charge of the contractors to be driven through by volunteer Indians, the remainder of the party, their wagons, beef, and corn were embarked December 23 on a small steamboat and two keel boats that carried them down the river to Waterloo; here they were placed aboard the steamboat Alpha and two large keel-boats in tow for the passage to Fort Gibson, and departed the twenty-sixth."*

The first contingent of Creeks removed along the Mitchell Trace, took only 13 days to travel from Wetumpka to Moulton. The old Mitchell Trace follows the route described above until it crosses the West Fork of Flint Creek approximately one mile north of the Oakville Indian Mounds Park. After crossing the Fish Dam Ford on West Flint, Mitchell Trace continues to Melton's Bluff while the old wagon road Coosa Path used by the removal contingent turns west toward Moulton.

It was along this route the Creek Indian people traveled to Moulton arriving there on December 19, 1835. Remnants of the old 'road to Moulton can be observed on County Road 186 approximately one-half of a mile south of Elam Creek. Again, the old road is visible where is crosses the Drag Strip Road on County Road 184 just one-fourth mile south of Elam Creek. The old road continues west toward Moulton and enters town near the Byler Road Fork and Pinhook Road Junction.

Again on September 5, 1836, a group of Creeks departed Tallassee in a wagon train that consisted of 45 wagons, five hundred ponies, and two thousand Indians. On September 24, 1836, the party camped at Town Creek, Alabama. This party utilized the same route as taken by the group in 1835. This large group of Creek Indians took 19 days to reach camp at Town Creek. The extra 6 days of travel was probably due to the extremely large size of the removal contingent. The Creek removal party probably passed through the Oakville Indian Mounds Park on September 22, 1836, since Oakville is some 25 miles from Town Creek.

Creek Resistance

There was much resistance to the removal of the Creeks. In 1829, the Creek National Council voted to stay in their ancestral homeland and submit to the laws of the State of Alabama. The Creeks did not want to leave the land where their ancestors were buried and they had heard reports of the great number of deaths of the Choctaws when they were removed. Eneah Micco, principal chief, and other chiefs from the Lower Creeks, protested to the secretary of war in the spring of 1831 the operation of law in Alabama over them. Because the oath of the Indian was not accepted in court, there was no legal redress when crimes were committed against them. *"The land grabbers used misrepresentation, the Indian not knowing what he was signing, the use of intoxicants, the misuse of notary seals on blank instructions to be filled in at the swindler's convenience, outright forgery, the bribing of some subservient Indians to impersonate the owner and sign in his place, and rigged probate procedure in the State courts corrupted by the general dishonesty to get title to Indian land"* (Debo, 1986).

On March 24, 1832, the Creeks signed the Treaty of Washington which ceded all of their five million acres of territory to the United States. This treaty reserved just over two million acres to be allotted to the Creeks. These parcels were to belong to individual Creeks who were to be given the deeds after they had occupied the land for five years. The U.S. government agreed to protect these Creek's lives and property and remove any white intruders. The U.S. agreed to pay the expenses of any Creek's removal to the West and finance their subsistence for their first year there. The Creeks were explicitly assured in the treaty that they were free to stay or to emigrate.

The United States broke the terms of the treaty within days. Whites invaded the Creek land-looting, burning, raping, and killing. Alabama continued making conditions so miserable for the Creeks so that they would choose to remove to the West. The Creeks were driven from their lands, destitute and starving, and often had family members murdered all with little forthcoming help from the Federal government. When the Federal marshals did try to enforce the treaty and prosecute the most flagrant violations, they were met with stiff opposition from the State government.

Tenskwatawa

The Shawnee brothers of Tenskwatawa and Tecumseh attempted to unite all Southeastern Indians against the invading Europeans.

In December of 1834, the first party of 630 Creeks left for the West. They began their march in December, traveling by way of Tuscaloosa, Columbus, Memphis, Little Rock and on to Tulsa. The Indians were poor, almost destitute of clothing, and the weather was unusually severe. The journey of three months resulted in the death of 161 Creeks.

Tecumseh

In May of 1836, in reprisal against the land speculators, bands of Lower Creeks began attacking white people and destroying their property between Tuskegee, Alabama and Columbus, Georgia. Alarmists feared that these reprisals were the beginning of another Creek War. This fear prompted the Secretary of War to order U.S. troops to Alabama to remove all Creeks by force. In July 1836, 2,498 Creeks (including 900 Yuchis) were put into two steamboats and taken down the Alabama River to Mobile and from there to Indian territory.

As the final group of Lower Creeks were preparing for removal, the Seminoles began hostilities and 700 Lower Creek men were called into service with the U.S. Army against the Seminoles. The families of these men were

123

placed in concentration camps where they were supposedly under the protection of Federal officers. These camps were attacked by mobs from Russell County, Alabama and Franklin County, Georgia. The mobs raped the women, killed some of the men, and carried off some the Indians into slavery. When some of the Creeks escaped into the swamps, the Alabama militia went in and killed many of them. In March 1837, four-thousand Creeks were collected at Montgomery to be sent by river to concentration camps at Mobile. The Creeks who fought the Seminoles were taken to Mobile where they joined what remained of their families in these camps.

The Creeks were loaded onto steamboats to be taken west. One of the steamboats, the Monmouth, collided with another boat and sank. Of the 611 Indians on board, 311 were drowned. By 1838, Creek removal was complete except for some who were held as slaves in Alabama and a very few others who had escaped removal (Foreman, 1986). Many mixed-blood Creeks were not removed and remained in the lands of the Warrior Mountains-the home they loved.

Chickasaw Indian Removal

The Chickasaw were determined not to sell their homeland and migrate west; however, two things happened to break their resistance. On May 28, 1830, the United States Congress passed the Indian Removal Act. The President was given the power to negotiate with the various tribes for their lands in any State or Territory in exchange for new lands west of the Mississippi River. The law committed the Federal government to compensate Indians for improvements on lands ceded, to bear removal cost, and provide emigrating tribesmen subsistence for one year after arrival in their new homes. Nothing new was produced by the Indian Removal Act since the U.S. government had been relocating eastern tribes for years. The act did consolidate and solidify an ever going policy--expressing in dramatic form the U.S. government's intent and procedure for the removal.

The other development which broke the Chickasaw's determination not to remove was the extension of Mississippi and Alabama state law. In 1820, Mississippi began the process of extending its jurisdiction over the Chickasaw Nation in such areas as the recovery of fugitive slaves. During 1829 and 1830, these states adopted comprehensive statutes which erased tribal government and destroyed the power of the office. Tribal leaders who exercised the functions and powers of their office were faced with a $1,000 fine and imprisonment. The statutes abolished tribal law and declared all Indians subject to State laws.

The Chickasaw leaders appealed to President Andrew Jackson to deliver them from the application of these laws and to give them the protection promised by the treaties with the United States. After Jackson rejected their appeal, the Chickasaw leaders were ready to negotiate. Federal officials exploited the Chickasaws' willingness to negotiate.

In late August 1830, the United States treaty commissioners, John A. Eator and John Coffee, summoned tribal leaders to Franklin, Tennessee. President Jackson came from the nation's capital to lend force to the proceedings by his presence and his address at the council. Even though the Chickasaws were defeated, Levi Colbert and twenty-one other Chickasaw leaders did not give in easily. They presented bold proposals in an attempt to get maximum benefits for their people and themselves. Their demands included an allotment of 160 acres for each Chickasaw man, woman, and child; compensation for improvements, livestock, and furniture which could not be removed; and a cash settlement for each head of family not choosing to take the allotment for him and his family. The demands by the Chickasaws were refused by the commissioners who felt the demands were unreasonable.

The Franklin Treaty was signed in September 1830. The treaty provided for the cession of the Chickasaw eastern homeland in return for a western home for the tribe. Each warrior, widow with a family, and each white man with an Indian family was entitled to a half section of land (320 acres). Single persons were entitled to a quarter section of land (160 acres). The United States agreed to pay the nation an annuity of $15,000 for twenty years. Levi Colbert and four other tribal leaders were to receive allotments of four sections each. Lesser leaders received allotments of one to two sections each. The United States agreed to pay the cost of the removal and to provide subsistence to the Chickasaws for one year in their new land.

As a decided advantage for the Chickasaws, the Franklin Treaty could not be ratified until the Chickasaws had traveled to the new territory and chosen the lands they wanted. Because they were hard to satisfy, the Chickasaw removal was delayed seven years (Gibson, 1971).

The Pontotoc Treaty, signed October 20, 1832, was the basic removal document providing for the cession of all tribal land east of the Mississippi. The tribal domain was to be surveyed and sold as public lands either at public auction or private sale. As leaders searched for a western home, each adult Chickasaw was assigned to a temporary home where he was to remain until the removal. Each single man, twenty-one and over, received one section. Each family of five persons and under received two sections. Each family of ten persons and over was assigned four sections. Families owning fewer than ten slaves received an additional half section; families owning over ten slaves received one section.

The Chickasaws were to be compensated for the improvements on the homesteads. Proceeds from the sale of vacated homesteads and surplus lands were to go to the Chickasaw Nation's general fund. From the proceeds, the government was to deduct the expenses for surveys and land sales. The Federal government agreed to advance funds to the Chickasaws to pay removal expenses and subsistence for one year after emigration; however, this expense was to be deducted from the land sales proceeds.

The Chickasaw leaders, who were not happy with the Pontotoc Treaty, spent much time between 1833 and 1837 traveling to Washington and the trans-Mississippi territory. The delegation which was sent to Washington in 1833, denounced Commissioner Coffee and charged that he took advantage of them when Levi Colbert, their principal spokesman, was deathly ill and unable to speak for them. They were concerned that the treaty contained no provision for orphans. They urged that the size of temporary homesteads be increased. The Federal officials refused to discuss amending the Pontotoc Treaty. However, the Chickasaws difficulty in finding a suitable home west of the Mississippi and their continued occupancy of allotments coveted by settlers caused the Federal government to be more receptive to Chickasaw demands for changes in the Pontotoc Treaty.

In May 1834, a Chickasaw delegation met with officials in Washington and negotiated an agreement which amended the Pontotoc Treaty. The size of the temporary homesteads was increased. As provided in the 1832 agreement, families of ten or more still received four sections; but families of at least five members but less than ten were to receive three sections, and families containing less than five members received two sections. Persons owning less than ten slaves were to receive an additional half section, while owners of ten or more slaves received an additional section. Orphans were to receive a half section each. A basic change was that title to the temporary homestead was granted in fee simple. Proceeds from the sale of surplus lands were to go into a general tribal fund held and invested in income-producing stocks by the United States government as provided in the Pontotoc Treaty. The cost of survey and land sales was charged to this fund by the Federal government; the Chickasaws were to pay their emigration expenses from this fund. The proceeds from the sale of temporary homesteads were to go to individuals allotted who were classed as competent (capable of understanding and managing their own affairs); otherwise, the proceeds were controlled by the tribal commission.

A.M.M. Upshaw of Pulaski, Tennessee, was appointed superintendent of the Chickasaws for removal and assigned a staff to assist him in evacuating the Chickasaws from Mississippi and Alabama. Lieutenant J.D. Seawright was sent to Cincinnati to contract for 1,300,000 rations. Each ration (the daily issue to an emigrating Indian) cost eight and one-half cents and consisted of one pound of fresh beef or fresh pork or three-fourths quart of corn or corn meal or one pound of wheat flour, and four quarts of salt for every one hundred emigrants. The rations were to be placed at depots along the Chickasaw emigration trail--200,000 rations were to be delivered to Memphis, the depot near Little Rock was to receive 100,000 rations, and Fort Coffee on the Arkansas River was to receive 1,000,000 rations. The War Department officials estimated that this quantity of subsistence would be enough to provide for the Chickasaws on the trail and for four months after the arrival in their new homes.

Upshaw met regularly with the Chickasaw leaders and developed an emigration plan. His plan called for each party of emigrating Chickasaws to be assigned a conductor, a physician, and a disbursing officer who had charge of the commissary train which transported subsistence stores between depots and who supervised the ration issue. Although Upshaw hoped to have one thousand Chickasaws enrolled and ready to leave by June 1, 1837, only about 450 Chickasaws responded to his call.

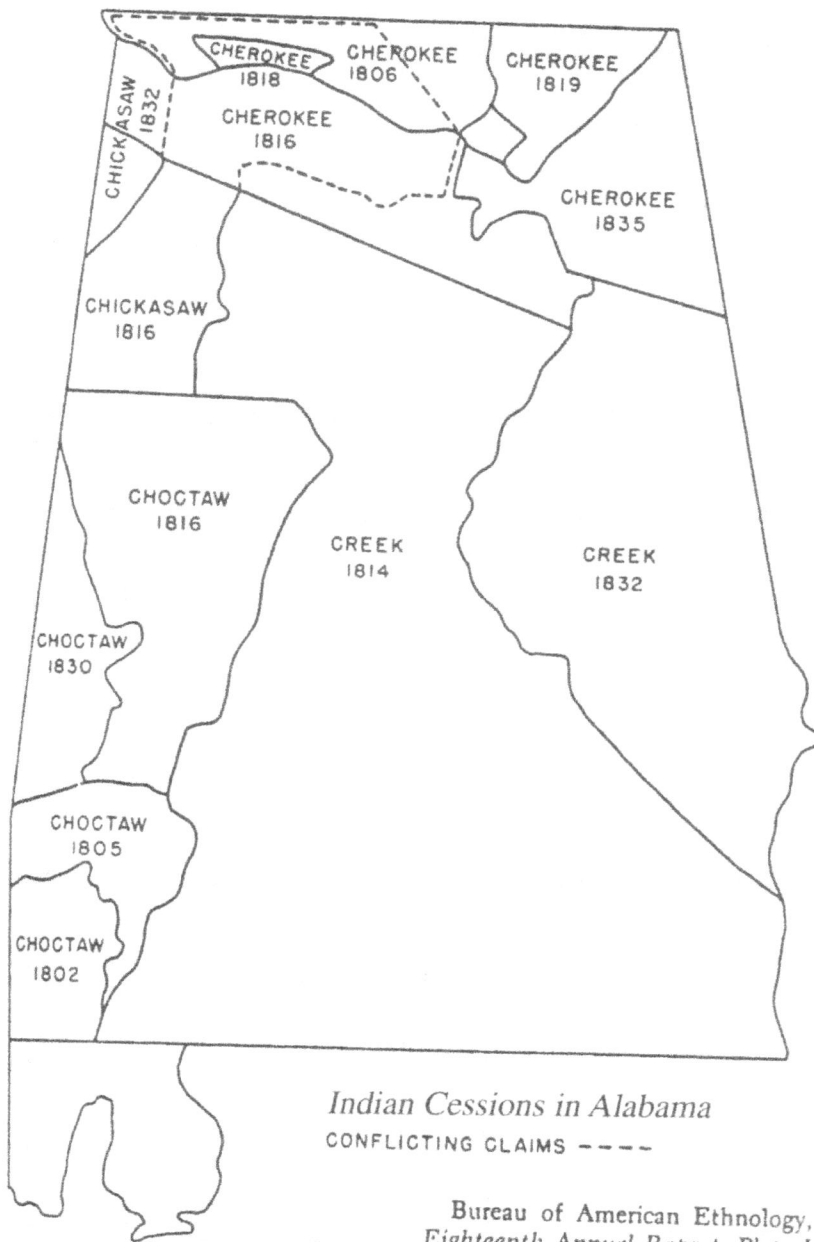

Indian Cessions in Alabama

CONFLICTING CLAIMS - - - -

Bureau of American Ethnology,
Eighteenth Annual Report, Plate I

Upshaw appointed John M. Millard the conductor for the first group to migrate west. They moved out in late June, and their long train was ferried across the Mississippi River from the Memphis landing on July 4. Heavy rains washed out the primitive Arkansas road causing the wagons to mire and sink to the axles. In their camps on high grounds, they were miserable because the water-soaked wood made fires for cooking and drying out clothing and bedding impossible. As the group traveled along the soggy trail, the number stricken with dysentery and fever increased each day. After the road dried out, Millard's party was able to average thirteen miles a day.

At the Little Rock depot, several late starting Chickasaws arrived and increased the size of the Chickasaw migration to almost five hundred. There Millard engaged steamers to transport the older people and the sick via the Arkansas River to Fort Coffee. Most of those who were able to travel decided to depart from Millard's route and to strike out southwesterly for the Choctaw settlements on the Red River near Fort Towson. Millard tried to get them to change their minds, but he finally ordered his disbursing officer, Lieutenant Governor Morris, to accompany them. After getting his group to Fort Coffee, Millard rushed off to join the group traveling to Fort Towson. This group traveled slowly for a number of reasons: fatigue, the number of ill increased, slowness in starting each day, and the number of rather increased.

Millard's compassion was submerged as his determination to achieve an "efficient and orderly movement" increased. On August 19, he spoke to the Indians accusing them of being ungovernable; then he issued an ultimatum to the tribal leaders. If the Indians did not choose to follow instructions, then within six days troops would arrive compelling the Indians to march at the point of the bayonet. The Chickasaw spokesmen agreed that the emigrants would comply. On September 5, this group of the first Chickasaw migrations arrived in the Choctaw settlement near Fort Towson (Gibson, 1971).

The first Chickasaw removal caused Federal officials to take firmer steps in removing the remainder of the Chickasaws. Before another party started west, the Chickasaw were to understand that they were to follow all rules and directions. They were not to deviate from the prescribed route; they were to go directly to Fort Coffee. If they refused to follow the course, Upshaw was directed to call for local troops to assist him. Removal officials were authorized to withdraw assistance including rations if they refused to cooperate.

During the summer and autumn of 1837, four thousand Chickasaws were enrolled and placed in four emigration camps in northwestern Alabama and northern Mississippi. Upshaw believed that he could get three-fourths of the Chickasaws started West by early November. He decided to move most of them by steamer and engaged Simeon Buckner, a Kentucky boatman, to transport the Chickasaws from Memphis to Fort Coffee for $14.50 per passenger. Baggage was to be loaded on flatboats and keelboats towed by the six steamers. The horse and cattle herds were to be moved by land with Indian drovers. In late October, the Chickasaw marched toward Memphis arriving at the landing on November 9. As they waited for the steamboats, Upshaw visited their camps and observed that only about five-hundred Chickasaws remained in Mississippi and that they would leave in the spring. Before the Chickasaws left on the steamers, news of a riverboat disaster involving several hundred Creek swept through the camps.

Although Upshaw was upset and threatened to withhold rations, only about one-thousand Chickasaws decided to travel by land. Konope, a spokesman for those choosing to go by land, said that since the Chickasaws were paying the emigration expenses that he doubted that drastic action could be taken. Upshaw gave in and proceeded to load those willing to go by water onto Buckner's steamer. He assigned conductors, physicians, and disbursing officers with a commissary train to the land-bound group.

Those Indians traveling by steamboat reached Fort Coffee in eight to ten days, while the other group traveling at a leisurely pace required a month to six weeks to reach the Arkansas River depot. Although most of the Chickasaws had arrived in the West by early 1838, small bands continued to emigrate every year for over a decade, and not until 1850 was the Chickasaw removal complete.

King Ishtehopa, the principal chief, arrived in June 1838 with 130 Chickasaws followed by 300 additional Indians the following year causing Upshaw to believe that the removal was complete. Upshaw then dismissed his conductors, physicians, and disbursing officers and reported to the commissioner of the Indian affairs that the Chickasaws were all west with the exception of eighteen to twenty families which he believed could remove themselves.

However, as late as April 1841, Federal officials in Mississippi reported that over 500 Chickasaws remained there.

After Upshaw's staff was dismissed, the Federal government adopted a policy of paying an emigration allowance of thirty dollars from the Chickasaw fund for each Indian or Chickasaw slave delivered to the Fort Coffee depot. Several enterprising Chickasaw mixed bloods took advantage of this policy. Some went into the emigration 'business by collecting scattered Chickasaw families and removing them to Indian Territory. Others drew the emigration allowance to reimburse themselves for expenses involved with overseeing their properties in Mississippi and Alabama There were certain Chickasaws who could not migrate West including a number of widows and orphans trapped in an exploitive web of Alabama and Mississippi state laws (Gibson, 1971).

As the removal took place, many of the emigrants faced unnecessary hardship. The government refused to abandon the contract system for providing goods and transportation to the Indians. The contractors were businessmen who were out to make a profit and contracts were issued that the lowest bidders. A.M.M. Upshaw, a Chickasaw agent, charged that com provided for the Chickasaw was so rotten even the horses refused to eat it. The haphazard planning of the Indian removal took its toll in human lives, because most of the removal took place during the winter months. The government's concern for economy worked against safe and healthy trips. The removal treaties promised medicine and physicians to the emigrants, but they were to be provided only when needed. Full medicine chests and surgical instruments were not purchased. There is evidence to indicate that the War Department conducted some inspections of goods and transportation vehicles, but continual emphasis on speedy removals, the strain on manpower caused by such inspections, and political pressure exerted by friends of the contracts, resulted in shortcuts and careless or infrequent examinations (Satz, 1979). Many Chickasaw mixed-bloods avoided removal and remained in North Alabama by claiming their white ancestry.

Choctaw Removal

The Choctaw Indians inhabited land in the southwestern comer of Alabama. After many attempts to move the Choctaws west of the Mississippi River, the Treaty of Doak's Stand in 1825, laid the groundwork for the Treaty of

Dancing Rabbit Creek. Five years later in 1830 the official removal of the Choctaws began and took three years to complete. The Choctaws were divided into three main districts and were moved largely by districts and kept their distinct districts after their removal.

Many descendants of Choctaws hid in the woods to escape removal. Many Choctaws settled on a Choctaw Indian Reservation near Philadelphia, Mississippi. Others were absorbed into the general population in Alabama and Mississippi. A large number of Choctaws, in Mobile and Washington Counties in Alabama, have reclaimed their heritage.

Modern Indians of the Warrior Mountains

The Modern Indian Tribes of Alabama

There are seven Indian tribes in the State of Alabama enrolling approximately 22,000 Indians. These represent about 13% of the 165,416 persons in Alabama who disclosed that they were of Indian ancestry in the Federal census of 1980. Most of those with Indian ancestry in Alabama are descendants of the Cherokee, Choctaw, and Creek tribes who were the aboriginal inhabitants of the State. The majority of the members of these tribes were removed to Indian Territory in the 1830's; however, a significant Indian minority remained in the State, including Cherokees in North and South Alabama, Creeks in South Alabama, as well as a sizable community of Choctaws in Southwest Alabama (Alabama Indian Affairs Commission, 1988).

The Mowa Choctaws of Southwest Alabama

The Mowa-Choctaw Tribe of Mobile and Washington Counties is recognized by most Alabamians as being the largest tribe in the state. There are about 35,000 Choctaws in the United States. There are over 10,000 in Alabama; of this number about 8,000 live in Washington and Mobile Counties. About 25,000 live in Mississippi and Oklahoma.

The name "Mowa" is a combination of the names of the two counties-Mobile and Washington-where most of them live. Because of inter-tribal and interracial marriages, the Mowa Band of Choctaws is a blend of Choctaws, Apaches, Kickapoo, and blacks. In December of 1981 in Washington County, the Choctaw Indians rekindled their first "great council fire" in more than 160 years in an attempt to bring the Choctaws together in the social, economic, and political challenges that face them today. Framon Weaver, Chairman of the Choctaw Commission, led his people in a rebirth of pride in their ancestry. Commission leaders wanted Alabama to recognize more than two races (black and white) and to have "American Indian" on their drivers licenses.

In June 1984, tribal people were selected to serve the Mowa Choctaws. Cleve Reed was elected tribal chairman. Each county elected two representatives. Prentiss Byrd and Charles K. Snow, Jr. represented Washington County. Elizabeth Cambell and Liza Sullivan represented Mobile County. Prentiss Byrd was elected as Tribal Treasurer. Russell C. Baker, Jr. was elected Executive Director of the Mowa Choctaws and has helped the tribe in their genealogy studies and application for Federal recognition. At the Choctaw Festival in McIntosh in December 1981, the Choctaw leaders announced that the tribe had filed suit asking for 240 acres of land that comprise most of the town of McIntosh and two major chemical plants. The suit was filed on behalf of Melton Snow who once owned the land. Defendants were the heirs of the late Representative Frank Boykin. Leaders say that other legal action will be taken later to reclaim part of 200,000 acres that some Choctaws say had been taken illegally by whites. John Rivers, a member of the Choctaw Commission, stated that the Choctaws were without legal counsel for years and that their lands had been taken by shrewd men using deceptive means. Rivers announced to the assembled guests that even though the festival was entertaining; its purpose was to dramatize the Choctaw heritage and to instill in the young the traditions of the Choctaws. Several politicians attended the event because of the political power of the Indian vote.

Chief Gallasneed Weaver, a past chairman of the Mowa Band, is an ordained Baptist minister and principal of Reeds Chapel Elementary School in McIntosh; and has worked for recognition (both State and National) for the Mowa Choctaws. With recognition came equal status with other tribes and voting rights in any Indian conference. Recognition would also mean free schooling at any

Indian college for tribal members and Federal assistance in housing and job markets to be provided through the Bureau of Indian Affairs.

Barbara Johnson is director for the Mowa Band of Choctaws. According to her, the Mowa Band is a non-profit organization dedicated to the betterment of the Choctaw. The Pow-Wows and festivals are their only means of supporting their tribal government and providing services to their Indian people. The festivals are designed to provide spectators with examples of the skills, artistry, and pride of their ancestors.

Today, the annual Mowa Choctaw Pow-Wow is held the third weekend of June drawing a large crowd of visitors from across the state. The scheduled events included the Choctaw Princess contest-the princess then represents the tribe at various events during the year. Other events include arts, crafts, Indian dances, and ceremonies.

The tribe of the Mowa Choctaw was incorporated in 1979 and is led by five officers and fourteen members of the tribes' commission who assist the operations of tribal affairs; today they have a good self-concept and are proud of their heritage as Native Americans.

Loretta Weaver, a Cherokee Indian from Stilwell, Oklahoma, serves as treasurer of the Mowa Council and teaches traditional Indian beading. She also directs the Mowa Indians Youth for Christ at two churches and the Mowa Dancers, who make appearances throughout the state. Her leadership and dedication to the Indian Education Project in Washington County caused Dr. Richard Snowden, Director of Title IV, to comment that the Mowa project in 1981 was one of the finest in the country and should be used as a model for other areas (Cromer, 1984).

The Cherokee of Northeast Alabama

The Jackson County Cherokees formed a Tribal Council on May 5, 1981, at North Sand Mountain High School, Higdon, Alabama. Dr. H.L. "Lindy" Martin presided over the meeting which elected the following council members: Jaynn Kushner, Ceil' Hicks, Bill Williams, Joe Hunkapiller, Marland Mountain, David Cornally and David Rooks. The presence of the Cherokee in Jackson

County was almost unknown for years even though the tribe had been under the leadership of Chief John Justice, William Keep, James McCony, and Claud Thornhill.

According to Dr. Martin the Cherokees of Jackson Alabama, are the descendants of the Cherokee Indians who were led by Chief Dragging Canoe. The Indians had come into Alabama in the early 1780's and settled in an area which had traditionally been tribal hunting territory. They established five major towns and several small villages.

Dr. Martin resigned as chairman of the Jackson County Cherokees in the fall of 1982. In 1983, the tribe changed its name to Cherokees of Northeast Alabama, Inc. Travis Staggs became Chairman, and David Rooks became Vice Chairman. In 1984, Jayne Kushner became representative to Alabama Indian Affairs Commission (Cromer, 1984).

The Echota Cherokee Tribe of Alabama

The United Cherokee Tribe of Alabama was organized on June 14, 1978, at Daleville, Alabama. B. J. Faulkner was elected principal chief. A council of nine people was formed, and the Secretary and Treasurer positions were filled.

In 1978, Chief Faulkner opposed the development plans for an industrial park near Northport that would disturb a 1,000 year old Indian village site and burial ground. In January of 1980, he sought the reburial of 3,000 Indians along the route to be flooded by the Tennessee Tombigbee Waterway. In 1980, disenchanted members of the United Cherokee Tribe of Alabama formed a new tribe called Echota Cherokee Tribe Inc. Joseph "Two Eagles" Stewart was elected principal chief, and letters of incorporation were filed in Shelby County and their seal was registered. The tribe filed for and received non-profit status and clans were organized over the State. A newsletter "Smoke Signals" was mailed to members. Regular monthly meetings were held at the Alabaster Community Center. The governing body of the tribe, consisting of tribal council members, elected officers, principal chief and vice-principal chief, was set in to serve a four year term (Cromer, 1984).

Some members of the Echota Cherokee.

Bobby Gillespie, former chief of the Blue Clan, Echota Cherokee

Billy Shaw, former Chief of Echota Cherokees of Alabama

Greg Preston

Terra Manasco

Lamar Marshall

The Echota Cherokee Tribe is the largest and one of the most active tribes in Alabama today. The tribe has approximately 16,000 members in Alabama and other states. The tribe is affiliated with five Title 4- A Indian Education Programs in Huntsville City Schools, Madison County, DeKalb County, Jackson County, and Lawrence County. The tribe has a land fund established for the purpose of purchasing land to build a Cherokee meeting ground and museum. The Echota Cherokee National Dance Team performs at Pow-Wows and festivals in Alabama and surrounding states. Tribal members are active in voter registration drives around the state. The tribe, represented by the principal chief, is a member of the Alabama Indian Affairs Commission and the National Congress of American Indian (Cromer, 1984).

The Ma-Chis Lower Creeks of Coffee County

In 1985, almost 900 Lower Creeks of Coffee County organized a tribe called Ma-Chis Creeks. The tribe was the first organized under the rules and guidelines of the Alabama Indian Affairs Commission. As the first elected woman chief in the United States, Mrs. Penny Wright was featured in three issues of <u>Woman's Day</u> magazine in 1985. Governor George Wallace appointed Dr. Johnny Wright, a high school principal in Pike County, to represent the tribe on the A.I.A.C. The tribe is affiliated with the Title IV Coffee County Indian Education Program (Cromer, 1984).

The Star Clan of Lower Muscogee Indians

The Star Clan of Creeks was organized in 1975 in Goshen, Pike County, Alabama under the name Eufaula Star Clan. The name Eufaula was chosen in honor of their ancestors, the Eufaula Indians of the area. Larry Johnson was appointed chief and papers of incorporation were filed in Pike County and with the Secretary of State. The tribe applied for a grant under the 1972 Indian Education Act. Following the appointment of Tommy Davenport as chief, the tribe changed its name to The Star Clan Lower Muscogee Tribe. The Star Clan is affiliated with the Lower Tribe of Muscogee. Of the more than' twelve hundred people known to be of Creek lineage in Pike County, only two hundred and fifty have chosen to declare their race through registration. The Indian Education Program has enrolled approximately 450 children of Creek ancestry. In 1981, the Star clan opened a crafts store in Frog, where Southeastern Indian crafts are sold on consignment. The Star Clan meets every other month in the town hall of Goshen unless the crowd is large then they meet at the Pike County Board of Education.

The Cherokees of Southeast Alabama

In 1982 in Houston County, a group of Cherokee Indians organized into a tribe under the leadership of their elected chief, Deal Wambles. In 1984, the tribe began efforts to establish Indian Education Classes in their county school system, where tribal members are taught Indian beadwork, dances, and leather work. In 1984, the Tribe held their Pow-Wow which drew members and guests from

Houston and Dale Counties. The tribal government is made up of an executive committee, the principal chief, the vice-principal chief, the administrative chief, the tribal council, the medicine man, the beloved woman, and the war chief (Cromer, 1984).

The Poarch Band of Creek Indians of Escambia County, Alabama

In 1941, Frank G. Speck, an American ethnologist, rediscovered the Creek Indians living at Poarch near the Town of Atmore in Escambia County, Alabama. According to local Creek Indian history, Lynn McGhee was a friendly Creek who served as a guide during the Creek War. The United States Government granted McGhee three remote parcels of land totaling 640 acres in Escambia and Baldwin Counties. Lynn's son, Richard, settled on the grant land which was to become Poarch. By 1900, a core of Creek families, characterized by strong patterns of in-group marriage, had become firmly established in western Escambia County on and around the McGhee grant land. In 1924, the U.S. Government which legally made the grant land taxable. However, title was acquired by only those heirs who paid local taxes; more of the land passed into the hands of non-Indians. Eventually all the land became individually owned and subject to property tax (Cromer, 1984).

Since the rediscovery of the Poarch Creeks in 1941, steps toward National recognition have been taken. In 1947, Calvin McGhee, a descendant of Lynn McGhee, organized an informal group of men to approach the county school board, the Governor, and other organizations to improve the Indian community (Cromer, 1984). In 1950, a council was formally organized to file a claim with the Indian Claim Commission (ICC) for payment of lands ceded by the Treaty of Fort Jackson in 1914. On January 5, 1951, the council moved to intervene in a suit brought by the Creek Nation of Oklahoma before the ICC, for recovery of such damages caused to the tribe as a result of the government's acquisition of Creek land under the Treaty of Fort Jackson.

In 1971, this council incorporated as a non-profit corporation under Alabama State law as the Creek Nation East of the Mississippi. In 1976, they organized the first secret ballot general election of a "tribal council" for the Creek Nation East of the Mississippi at their annual Thanksgiving Pow-Wow. By 1978 the variety and scope of State and Federally funded programs at Poarch had

141

dramatically expanded, far beyond the level of 1976. In February of 1980, four representatives of the Poarch Band of Creeks met in Washington, D.C. with Senator Howell Heflin, Donald Stewart and Representative Jack Edwards of Mobile, to discuss their petition to the Department of Interior for Federal recognition of their tribe.

On August 16, 1980, at Fort Toulouse, the Creek Nation East of the Mississippi (Poarch Band) accepted a deed of ownership of a 33 acre site known as Ocheo-Pofare, or the Hickory Ground, where the headquarters of the entire Creek Nation was located during the early 1800's. The Poarch Band of Creeks has received some federally funded programs through OEO, the Indian Education Act of 1972, and a federal grant to the Coalition of Eastern Native Americans (CENA). Representative Jack Edwards, R., Mobile, who pushed for Federal recognition for the Poarch Creeks for 19 years, told 6,000 people gathered for the 13th annual Creek Pow-Wow in Poarch on Thanksgiving Day, 1983, that the Department of Interior reviewed the seven criteria for "nation status" and determined the Creek tribe qualified.

On August 11, 1984, the United States Government's Department of Interior, Bureau of Indian Affairs acknowledged the Poarch Creek Tribe as the first and only federally recognized tribe in the State of Alabama. On June 1, 1985, the tribe adopted their own constitution. A none-member tribal council was elected to govern the tribe.

The State of Alabama saw the first federally recognized Indian tribe as a potential tourist attraction. The original tribal land had swindled to about 17 acres when the State assisted the Creeks in acquiring 264 acres of land alongside Interstate 65 near Atmore. On November 21, 1984, 231.54 acres of Creek land was placed in federal trust. In 1985, the Poarch Creeks built a Bingo Palace on their reservation and purchased a nearby motel and restaurant as a business investment (Cromer, 1984). On April 12, 1985, 229.54 acres were declared a Reservation.

The Poarch Band of Creeks recognizes members Eddie Tullis, Dale Gehman, Larry Haikey, and Bill Smith in addition to many others. Eddie Leon Tullis, of Atmore, Alabama, who became tribal chairman in 1978, led the Poarch Band of Creek Indians in their petition to the United States Government to recognize a government-to-government relationship with the Poarch Band of Creeks. Tullis serves as chairman of the Tribal Council of the Poarch Band of, Creeks, and as Vice-President of the National Congress of American Indians (NCAI). He serves as a member of the Human Resource Committee of the Congress, and continues to lead organized efforts to increase and improve the social and economic situation of the Poarch Creeks.

Dale Gehman is the chief engineer general manager of WASG radio station owned by a Creek Indian family. Gehman's father, two brothers, and mother fill various positions at WASG, the Spirit of the Gulf Coast. WASG, the second Indian owned commercial radio station, began operating November 12, 1981. Larry Hoikey, the tribal planner in charge of obtaining Federal grants and loans, has been instrumental in getting Creek Indian handcrafts into the marketplace. Creek "ribbon shirts" are the most popular item. Quilts, blouses, pillows, potholders, and cushions are made for market by the Creeks at their new sewing center.

Bill Smith, vice-chairman of the Poarch Band of Creeks, appeared in the "First Frontier" which tells a 300 year story spanning early Spanish exploration to the State to the Trail of Tears in the 1830's. Bill Smith had appeared in documentary films, television programs and visited schools on behalf of Poarch Band of Creek Indians. He has also worked with the Alabama Forestry Commission in a campaign to prevent forest fires. His ambition is to become Alabama's Iron Eye (Cromer, 1984).

Politics Relating to Alabama Indians

President Andrew Jackson secured passage of the Indian Removal Bill which was enacted into law on May 28, 1830. Greed for lands which belonged to the Southern Indians was Jackson's motive for promoting the congressional act that took away and abolished all the rights, privileges, immunities, and franchises held, claimed, or enjoyed by those persons called Indians. Jacksonian politics against Indian people lead to the darkest blot in history for the American government.

Cataclysmic changes in Indian lifestyle caused by the government's policies toward the Southern Indians created an environment of fear, desolation, suffering, hardship and grief brought about by thousands of tragedies that occurred to Indian people throughout Alabama. The mixed-blood Indian (people that remained in the Warrior Mountains of North Alabama after removal were afraid of the laws and policies of the State and Federal government. These people were proud of their Indian ancestry, but due to fear did not claim their Indian heritage. They did not list themselves as Indians in census records until opinion and laws concerning Indian people begin to change.

The year 1924 was a turning point for most American Indians, when all Indians were made citizens of the United States. Since anti-Indian discrimination remained throughout the U.S., most Southern Indian people east of the Mississippi did not benefit by this law. By 1924, most Indian ways and culture of Lawrence County's mixed-blood Indian people were lost. These people were absorbed into the general population and totally adapted to white ways. Both local and state laws, relatively unaffected by the 1924 Citizenship Law, still discriminated against all minorities including Indian people.

In 1943, the National Congress of American Indians was established. The organization eventually grew to include some ninety tribes containing two-thirds of the Nation's Indians. The goals of the Congress were two-fold. It wanted Indians to have the same civil rights white Americans have. It wanted Indians on reservations to be allowed to retain their own customs and values, even if those were different from the customs and values of mainstream society. The Echota Cherokee Tribe of Alabama became an active member of the National Congress of American Indians.

On July 2, 1964, President Johnson signed the most sweeping piece of civil rights legislation since Reconstruction. The new law gave all citizens, regardless of race, the right to enter such public facilities as libraries, parks and washrooms. It forbade discrimination in restaurants and theaters. One of the most important congressional acts involving Indian Civil Rights legislation included Titles II-VII of the Civil Rights Act of 1968 which was enacted into law on April 11, 1968.

Alabama's mixed-blood Indian community, in reclaiming their Indian heritage, began to reorganize their tribes. With organization, Indian people in Alabama worked to improve State laws through legislation. The State of

Alabama has passed laws which helped Indian people in the state. It is the Indian Self-Determination Act of 1975 that most Indian tribes, bands, and groups in Alabama have turned to for legal definitions of their status as Indians or tribes.

The passage of the Mims Act in the regular legislative session of Alabama on May 3, 1978, and subsequent formation of an Alabama Indian Affairs Commission (A.I.A.C) came as a climax to years of piece-meal legislation aimed at helping Indians in the state. The purpose of the Mims Act and the formation of an AIAC may have been an effort on the part of Alabama legislators to correct some of those past mistakes. The Mims Act was a direct result of the Fort Mims Massacre at the hands of the Upper Creeks at the beginning of the Creek Indian War. The Mims Act created the Southwest Alabama Indian Affairs Commission; provided for its duties and membership; prescribed the method of appointment and compensation of said commission; and repealed all laws or parts of laws that conflicted with this act.

The Davis-Strong Act repealed the Mims Act of 1978 and was passed on May 1, 1984. Funding in the amount of $125,000 was set aside for the New Commission which opened its office in Montgomery at 339 Dexter Avenue. The Commission immediately turned its attention the drafting of by-laws and budget allocations. Through the passage of the Davis-Strong Act, each of the six tribes in the State became automatically State recognized tribes, although recognition had already been given to the Poarch Band of Creeks with the passage of the Mims Act of 1978 (Cromer, 1984).

The following relates to Federal regulations which govern Indian Education Programs. To date there is no one Federal or tribal definition that establishes a person's identity as Indian. Anyone who declares himself to be an Indian is considered an Indian by the Bureau of the Congress. The U.S. Department of Labor defines an Indian as a person having origins in any of the original people of North America, and who maintains cultural identification through tribal affiliation or community recognition.

The following are the provisions of the Indian Education Act of 1975 (Public Law 92-318): The term Indian means any individual who; is a member of a tribe, band, or other organized group of Indians including those tribes, bands, or others terminated since 1940 and those recognized by the State in which they reside, or who is a descendant in the first or second degree, or any such member or, is considered by the Secretary of the Interior to be Indian for any purpose or, is an Eskimo, or Aleut or other Alaska native or, is determined to be an Indian under regulations promulgated by the Commissioner, Advisory Council on Indian Education.

Alabama Indian Affairs Commission

The Alabama Indian Affairs Commission is the state agency that represents Indian people in the State of Alabama. The commission serves more than 24,000 American Indians represented by seven tribes, bands, or groups and works to improve the quality of life for Indian people throughout the state.

In May of 1984, Governor George Wallace signed into law the Davis-Strong Act creating the Alabama Indian Affairs Commission. The AIAC represents seven tribal groups of American Indians who are citizens of Alabama. The following commissioners were appointed by Governor George Wallace: Gallasneed Weaver, Mowa Choctaws; Tommy Davenport, Pike County; Creeks, Tom Hutto, Echota Cherokee; Jayne Kushner, Cherokee of Northeast Alabama; Deal Wambles, Cherokee of Southeast Alabama; Eddie Tullis, Poarch Band of Creeks. Roger Creekmore of Tuscumbia was appointed to represent "at large", or non-tribally affiliated Indians' in the state. Loretta Pittman of Crossville was appointed to represent federally recognized Indians on the AIAC. Gallasneed Weaver was elected chairman; Tommy Davenport was elected vicechairman. Jane Weeks is the Executive Director, Darla Graves represents TERO (Tribal Economic Resource Officers).

The duties and responsibilities of the Alabama Indian Affairs Commission are set forth in five brief statements.

(1) Voicing concerns and issues of Indian People.
(2) Promoting the right to pursue cultural and religious traditions.
(3) Assisting in social and economic development of all Indian Communities.
(4) Seeking aid and protection of Indian rights.
(5) Pursuing meaningful programs for Indian citizens (Cromer, 1984).

Indian Stories of the Warrior Mountains

Cherokee Stories

'Principal People' Survived Defeat
The Decatur Daily, September 13, 1964, by John Knox.
Origin of Cherokee Name Hazy

Nobody knows for certain where the name "Cherokee" originated. It may derive from "Acheoloque," as their mountain province was called in the De Soto narratives. Or it may have been conferred upon them by the Muskhogean tribes, whose word, "Tciloki" means: "People who speak a different language." The Cherokees themselves finally adopted this work, in the form: "Tsalagi." Their preferred name, self-conferred, was "AniYuniya" meaning "Principal People." They had a reasonable claim to the title. They were not only the largest tribe of the Iroquois-North America's most important Indian group-but they were personally both talented and impressive.

William Bartram, the botanist, who traveled among them in the early 1770's, described them as superior in intelligence, and grave and lordly in manner. Their women were light colored and tall, in contrast to the squaws of the Creeks and the Choctaws, and the braves were the biggest men of any race that Bartram had ever seen.

PROWESS

Nobody disputes their prowess as warriors. But in the art of wholesale larceny, the paleface topped them. Cortez and Pizarre had set a record in Central and South America, and De Soto, less successful; nevertheless maintained the high standard of rapacity. But it remained for the Anglo Saxon to really raise the art of land-thievery to its ultimate refinement.

This took place, not on the battle field, where the crusty old "Indian-fighters" at least risked life and limb in a sporting contest, but in the legislative halls and land offices. Here grubby entrepreneurs, spouting pieties and tobacco juice, cooked up the witch-brew of legalistic humbuggery which robbed a race of its birth-right and left a stench in the air which endures to this day.

There was, of course, on the squatter level, the simple drive of a people seeking homes-an explosive pressure no more amenable to moral restraint than the head of steam which bursts a boiler. You can't indict a historic process, but you can deplore ignoble methods, and meaner ones were never employed. Yet there had been early traders, trappers, adventurers, who loved the Indian's freedom and closeness to nature. Often they proved his staunchest allies. Scotchmen were conspicuous among these, perhaps because, like the Cherokees themselves, the Scots were highlanders.

CHAMPIONS

In times before the Revolution, John Stuart and Alexander Cameron, agents of the Crown, were champions of the Cherokee's cause. Hawkins, McKee, and Gaines were U.S. agents friendly to the Indians. Ross and Gunter and Vann are names conspicuous in early North Alabama annals- not to mention the famous Scotch chieftains among the Creeks, farther south.

Eleazer ("Old Rabbit") Wigan was with the Overhill Cherokees as early as 1711. Later came David Dowie, William and Joseph Cooper, Robert Bunning, Ludovic Grant. The latter, from a highland clan ruined in the lost cause of James II, became a man of great influence among the Cherokees. James Adair, who wrote his theories of the "Lost Tribes" while among the Chickasaws, was a visitor among the "Principal People" too.

But the Scotch family we are most interested in at the moment is that of the Vanns, who founded a dynasty which survived the tragic "Removal." We know a descendant of this Scotch-Indian family. He is Maurice Vann, a pharmacist of Decatur, and he may just possibly be the only Cherokee "medicine man" still practicing in the Tennessee Valley. Maurice is a descendant of James Vann, a chief and the father of "Rich Joe" Vann, who operated a plantation with an imposing mansion and engaged in business ventures which extended from his estate at Spring Place, Georgia. At one time he owned the first steamboat which ever came across the Shoals.

Cherokees engage in a game.

Maurice did not know about that steamboat-a piece of information we picked up studying riverboat history-but he furnished documents and family reminiscences and records. Incidentally, his descent from James Vann makes him a cousin (at some remove) to the late Will Rogers, who seems to have been related to the Vann and the Gunter families.

WILL ROGERS, JR.

In the publication, "Early Georgia" (Spring, 1957), president D. B. Bandy, of the Whitfield-Murray Co. Historical Society, mentions a letter from Will Rogers, Jr., in 1948, stating that his grandfather was Clement Vann Rogers, of Spring Place. His great-grandfather is presumed to be Clement Vann II, who built "Vann House."

149

In the same publication, Clements de Baillou states that the first Clement Vann entered the Cherokee territory at some time during the second half of the 1700's. There is a tradition that he belonged to the Scotch nobility, but at any rate it seems certain that he came west from Charleston, South Carolina., and it is thought that he first established a trading post south of Gainesville, Georgia, on Chestnut Hill Road.

Later he went into the territory beyond the mountains, married the daughter of a Cherokee chieftain, and became Town Chief of the settlement. "His son James," de Baillou continues, "must have been born about 1770, and he became the most important figure in the Vann family." He is said to have supported Christian civilization as a means of progress for the Cherokees.

In 1809, James Vann killed a tribesman in a duel, and in 1809 he was in turn killed by a relative, in accordance with the old tribal law. His will, probated in the Jackson County court, bequeathed to his wife, Peggy, his household furniture, and all the residue of his estate to his son, Joseph. This European practice of primogeniture, however, was not an Indian institution, and the council of chiefs voided the will and distributed the property between the widow and the children, but will allowed Joseph the largest share.

COUNCIL MEMBERS

The names of the council members affixed to this decree are: "Rabbit, John Beamer, Noon Day, Cotaquarkee, The Chip, Waman's Nephew, Oclahetta, Chatloe, Path Killer, The Boots, Sam Mush, Rushing Fawn, Tusquokeukee, The Bug, The Hawk, and Going Snake."

Small wonder the Jackson County court upheld the decree of such an impressive aggregation.

With Joseph (Rich Joe) Vann, we come into the full light of history. He was born on February 11, 1798. His Cherokee name was Teautle. He took good care of his inheritance and became a very rich man. But at the time of the "Trail of Tears," when 13,000 Cherokees were rounded up like cattle and shipped in "floating doggeries" down the river, to entrain at Decatur for the trip west, Joe Vann suffered privation and indignity, too.

Cherokee Chief John Ross

Writing of those parlous times, Donald Davidson, historian of the Tennessee River, says: "not even the highest chiefs, in fact, escaped molestation. John Ross's Georgia estate was seized by Georgia authorities under the lottery law, and the holder of the ticket for Ross's lands gained possession of his farm, his house and his ferry at the head of the Coosa River. Mrs. Ross, who was in bad health, was allowed to remain on the ground floor, but Ross had to seek refuge in Tennessee.

"Joseph Vann, house worth $10,000, was even more grossly mistreated. His property was seized by the Georgia militia on a trumped-up charge. But there were rival claimants to his property. A man named Spencer Riley took possession of the upper part of the house, armed to defend his claim. When W.N. Bishop, commander of the Georgia guard, entered the lower part, the two groups of white men staged a battle in the house, while Vann and his family sought to escape the flying bullets.

SMOKED HIM OUT

"Riley, though wounded, would not give up. Thereupon Bishop set fire to the house, smoked him out, and obtained possession. Vann and his family fled through the snow to seek refuge in a log cabin across the Tennessee line."

After this and other equally admirable performances by the race which "brought Christianity to the Indian," it was no small tribute to Joe Vann's enterprise that he managed to survive and even hang onto some of his wealth. We know that he had enough left to buy a steamboat-the famous Holston, which had first attempted regular crossings of the shoals, but which had not proved a financial success to her owners.

Renamed the Kingston, this boat was used to transport members of the Vann and Ross families down the river and toward the west.

Joe Vann settled at Webber's Falls on the Arkansas river and adopted the hobby of steamboat racing.

He either re-named the Kingston, or bought another boat, for the one he raced on the Arkansas was called the "Lucy Walker," and it was the cause of his death. An overheated boiler exploded and killed him, near Louisville, Kentucky, in 1844.

ELUDED PERSECUTORS

Several thousand Cherokees manage to elude their persecutors and remain in their homeland. White settlers helped some, others, like those on the Qualla Reservation, held out stubbornly until they were finally permitted to remain.

Other descendants of James Vann, who did not accompany "Rich Joe" to Arkansas, settled on Sand Mountain, in Forrest Home community near Boaz in Marshall County. These included William Jasper Vann, and Alfred Vann. John Wesley Vann, the father of Maurice Vann, of Decatur was born at the homestead there. Later John Wesley moved to Union Hill, where Maurice was born. Vann relatives still live on Sand Mountain and in Birmingham.

Though their Indian blood had been considerably diluted through the years, the Vanns still proudly claim a share in the courageous Indian tradition.

A Cherokee girl in ceremonial dress.

Cherokee History is our Lost Horizon

Indian May Be Oldest Distinct Race
The Decatur Daily, September 9, 1964
by John Knox

At least as early as World War I, the hill-rimmed eastern section of the Tennessee Valley boasted an arsenal. Now that rocketry has come to dominate all forms of armament, Huntsville, with its space center, may fairly be considered THE arsenal of America. Less known is the fact that at least two centuries earlier;

this same general region was one of the prime seats of military power for our predecessor, the Indian.

"The mountainous eastern part of the Tennessee Valley, where the Cherokees lived," says Donald Davidson, in The Tennessee, was in fact the inner citadel of the Indian race in the country east of the Mississippi line.

Before the Cherokee, there were, of course other tribes and if the Huntsville rockets were actually launched from there, like giant arrows toward the moon, the fiery feathers which tip their shafts would cast a glare over the haunts of tribe receding into the blue mists of 15 millenniums.

Cherokees Came

"Rock House", on the very edges of the Redstone Reservation, was a home of "Copena" people centuries before the Cherokees came. We know them only by their artifacts. But the Cherokee, in a measure, is still with us. He is our link with past ages; his culture merges with ours on the valley's historic horizon. He was the last in this region of an ethnological group who may be the oldest distinct, race on earth. For only the Amerindian, anthropologists say, can be identified as a homogenous species as long as 200 centuries ago.

Considering this, it becomes almost unbelievable that the members of a race cut off from Old World culture since Paleolithic times, could have, in the space of a few decades, adapted themselves to the white man's way of life. The Cherokees leaped so swiftly across this barrier of the centuries that some students have tried to explain it by hypothecating an admixture with wandering Europeans long before the Spaniards came.

But whether this theory is considered possible or pure moonshine, most authorities agree that the people who called themselves "Ani- Yunwiya, Principal People," were different. Lewis and Newburg, in their survey of The Tribes that Slumber, state: "The Cherokee are not easily identified with any of the prehistoric cultures of the Southwest," and "The Cherokee language, which is related to Iroquois, is so dissimilar from Iroquois that linguists believe that the two peoples had been separated for a very long time."

Important Grouping

This Iroquoian stock, says John Collier, in The Indians of America is the most important Indian grouping on the continent north of Mexico. And of the Iroquoian Confederacy, he remarks: "I think no institutional achievement of mankind exceeds it in either wisdom or intelligence-accepting the limits of its time and place."

This league of five tribes was formed just 50 years after Columbus discovered America, and 50 years before Jamestown and Plymouth Rock. It was forged not merely as a deterrent to local strife, but with the ideal of achieving a universal and perpetual peace. And it operated successfully for 200 years.

The Cherokees, though not a member of the Confederacy, were the largest Iroquoian tribe, and they readily formed alliances with the British. When the Revolution had become an accomplished fact, they made a treaty with the United States, and kept it as a strict and sacred duty. "The Cherokees," says Collier," met every test of peacefulness, of practicality, of Christian profession and conduct, of industry and productiveness, of outgoing friendliness to the whites, of progress in domestic order and education."

As early as 1721, the Cherokees had begun ceding land, and this proved equivalent to spooning out blood to a tiger. The process continued until their heritage was devoured. They were betrayed, tricked, cheated and finally driven out, after the infamous treaty of New Echota, in 1835.

Various Stages

The various stages of this process, the ramifications of double-dealing and chicanery-which aggravated occasional flare-ups on the Indians' part-is a long and sordid story. The pressure of white settlers from three sides kept compressing the Cherokee lands pushing them southwestward into an area stretching from eastern Tennessee through western North Carolina, northwest Georgia, and northeastern Alabama. Here, under stress, the Cherokees showed their remarkable resourcefulness and resilience. In a sense they re-made their lives, and they did it brilliantly.

From rudimentary agricultural practices they adapted to full-time farming as game supplies played out, building cabins, barns, and even mansions. They built schools and roads and churches. They formed their own government; having a legislature, a judiciary and an executive branch. They became plantation operators, business men, preachers, statesmen, and even newspapermen.

An 1824 census conducted by their own government showed that a total population of about 15,000 Cherokees owned some 1,000 slaves, 22,400 cattle, 7,600 horses, 40,000 swine, 3,000 sheep, 1,850 spinning wheels, 2,445 plows, 475 goats, 700 looms, 120 wagons, 20 grist mills, 55 blacksmith shops, 6 cotton gins, 10 ferries, and 9 stores.

But the most remarkable of all their achievements was the invention of an alphabet, or more correctly a syllabary, by the half-breed George Gist, or Sequoyah, whose monument may still be seen in Jackson County between Larkinville and Limrock. Born in 1760, the son of a Virginian, Nathaniel Gist, who married the sister of a Cherokee chief, he began his career as a silversmith. Though he could neither read nor write, he was fascinated by the idea that thoughts could be communicated by mere marks on paper.

Considered A Fool

Considered a fool by his family, he first attempted to devise signs for complete sentences. Next he tried symbols for words. Finally he broke the works into syllables and found 84 characters which could express all the sounds in the Cherokee language.

He utilized some German letters copied from the books of Moravian missionaries, combined them with others from an English Bible, modified them by turning them in various directions and adding strokes and curlicues, plus symbols of his own invention.

The system was a complete success. The leading men of the nation accepted his invention, and within a few months almost the entire Cherokee nation became literate. A newspaper -The Cherokee Phoenix, was founded and published for several years until the bitter agitation for a complete removal of the Indians resulted in the destruction of the presses and the arrest of the printer.

This agitation ushered in one of the blackest chapters in American history. Andrew Jackson, the Georgia politicians, the greedy land speculators, are all held to blame, and rightly. But seen in impersonal perspective, it was the result of the fact that the Cherokees stood like a rock in the natural path of one of the great folk movements in American history.

Sequoyah

Main Valley

This current would, unobstructed, have come southward down the main valley and up the tributary valleys of the Holston-Tennessee River systems.

The Cherokees split this tide and the Great Bend was settled partly from the Deep South, partly from middle Tennessee, on its north, and a long time before the land between the Chattanooga and the Hiwassee River was cleared of Indians. The "island" settlements in Tennessee were reached usually by the difficult "Wilderness Road" through the Cumberland Gap.

The Cherokees, a stubborn barrier, exerted a great influence on the culture of the infant states so long as they were able to hold out. But inevitably they were doomed by the glacier-like pressure of the migrating impulse. Meanwhile, they found some friends and helpers among the race who dispossessed them.

From earliest times, traders and adventurers, notably John Ross, John Gunter, and Joseph Vann, married into the tribe and became chiefs. Other friends were certain agents of the federal government such as Colonels Benjamin Hawkins and Return J. Meigs. Both were Indian agents who participated in tribal councils, took the Indians' side in disputes, distributed farming and household implements, gave medical aid, warded off intruders and encouraged the missionaries. These latter included Moravians, Presbyterians, Methodists, Baptists and others. They founded schools to which the Cherokees flocked.

It is this eagerness to learn, plus the capacity to equal the white brother in his own fields, which makes so pathetic and shameful the rejection of the Cherokee by a race who might have profited greatly by his contribution of wisdom, stamina, courage, and sensitivity to spiritual values. In another article we will consider the tragic expulsion-called the "Trail of Tears"- and delve into some individual histories of Cherokees who number among their descendants such men as Will Rogers, and many well-known and useful citizens of North Alabama.

Were The Cherokees 'Red Welshmen'?

800 Years of History Give 'Proof'
The Decatur Daily, August 19, 1964 by John Knox

A few days ago we were asked, "What do you make of all these red-headed, blue-eyed Cherokee Indians you hear about?"

We gave the usual easy answer: that traders were in the Alabama wilds long before the settlers came. Many became "countrymen", married Indian squaws, joined the tribes. Many-if not most of these- were Scots or kindred Gaels.

We finished with a shrug-that was for what was left unsaid. There is another hypothesis. We heard it as long ago as our first discovery of Southey's poem, "Madoc." But it's a controversial theory, scorned by most historians. It goes back to the great geographer, Hakylut, born in 1552. It goes further-to Wales, in 1170.

But the great George Catlin, a master portrayer of Indian life, believed it-on the basis of personal 'observation. And there have been many others who defended it. Consider this story which appeared in "The Public Advertiser," of Louisville, Ky. in May, 1819:

Berated Waiter

Lt. Joseph Roberts, a Welshman, born and reared in Wales, was dining in a Washington restaurant. The waiter who served him was of the same nationality. So, when his glass of water turned out to be warm, the lieutenant joking berated the waiter in Welsh. An Indian chief, who happened to be in the room, heard the words and came to Robert's table; he asked if the words he had overheard were in the officer's language.

Answered in the affirmative, he said that the language was his also, and in reply to Roberts' questions added that his tribal traditions said that his people had come from "a far distant country, very far in the east, and from over the great waters." He further stated that all the children of his tribe were accustomed to speaking only Welsh until they were 12-years old. Only then did they learn to speak other languages. The astonished officer later declared that the Indian spoke better Welsh than he did.

If this had been an isolated occurrence, it might have been readily dismissed. But stories of "Welsh Indians" and "White Indians" were rife on the frontier south of the Ohio. In the region around Louisville, Kentucky, it was accepted as fact that such a tribe had lived there.

Sacred Object

A certain William Sutton claimed to have lived with an Indian tribe "who dwelled a great distance above New Orleans", and who kept as a sacred object an old Welsh Bible. They were described as "not so tawny as other Indians ... and they spoke Welsh." Captain Isaac Stewart, of South Carolina, in an article published in 1787, reported that he had encountered a Welsh-speaking Indian tribe in 1771. He said they possessed parchment scrolls with strange writing and claimed that their forefather had come from a distant land to the east.

An even earlier Virginian, Morgan Jones, in 1660 wrote of his travels in North Carolina and the Kentucky area. He was captured by the Tuscarora (a branch of the Iroquoian stock to which the Cherokees also belonged.)

When he learned that his captors had decided to kill him, Jones burst into mournful protests in his native Welsh. Hearing this, an Indian approached, and addressed him in the same language. He was presently released, treated as a guest, and remained, preaching to these Indians in Welsh for four months. Whether these incidents prove anything or not, others besides Catlin have supported the Welsh Indian theory. Robert Durret, of Louisville, whose research was published in 1908 by the Filson club, was a supporter. He bolstered the theory with a story of skeletons dug up on nearby Sand Island, along with brass plated shields which bore the mermaid and harp of the Welsh coat of arms.

Never Returned

And who were these ancient Welshmen who had mingled their blood with the Indians of Kentucky? Why, they were the followers of Prince Madoc, who, in 1170 had left his native land became a dispute had arisen over the throne of his father, Own Gwynedd, had sailed to the West, discovered a new land, returned to recruit colonists, sailed off again with 10 ship-loads of followers-and had never returned to Britain.

Hakluyt's version of the story was published in 1582, and was said to be based on records found in two ancient abbeys in Wales. It has been kicked about and debated for eight centuries. A modern day supporter of the theory is Charles Michael Boland, whose book, "They All Discovered America: recounts the evidence in favor of Madoc's expedition-as well as that of other pre-Columbian discoverers.

He prints a map, constructed on the theories of Catlin and others, which shows the Welshman's ship skirting Florida, sailing up the Mississippi into the Ohio, and founding a settlement on Sand Island, near Louisville. He believes that proof might be found by excavating there.

And how do the Cherokees fit in? Well, Catlin believed that, after living for a century on the Ohio in Kentucky, the Welsh suffered a massacre by wild tribes, and that the remnant of their settlement moved up the Missouri river and became, in time, the Mandans-a word he derives from "Madawgwys," the name applied by the Welsh to the followers of Madoc.

Tuscaroras

But the century they spent in Kentucky, was in the territory of the Tuscaroras, an Iroquoian tribe akin to the Cherokees who were also in Kentucky, as well as Virginia, the Carolinas, Georgia, Tennessee, and later, Alabama. A lot of inter-mixing could have taken place during that 100 years, and certainly the Cherokees, like the now vanished Mandans, were a peculiar and "different" type of Indian, and in more ways than their oft noted physical appearance. The Creeks, Chickasaws and Choctaws, for example all showed definite influences from the great cultures of Mexico. The Cherokees did not." Among the Indians of the South," says Donald Davidson, in "The Tennessee," "the Cherokees were a somewhat peculiar and separate people." He notes that their myths differed from the others, and says "they were the quickest of all the Indians to assimilate the white man's civilization."

They adopted the white man's agricultural economy and political institutions and published a newspaper. They invented an alphabet "No other Indians on the continent, "Davidson remarks," displayed exactly this kind of genius."

Like the Scotch and Welsh, they were mountaineers. They liked to live with "a mountain at their back and a river in their front," Davidson notes. So did the white pioneers who, having left the sand and pine belt of Virginia and the Carolinas, found the Cherokee country of Tennessee, Alabama and Georgia, "desirable beyond compare."

Hence the often bitter conflict between Indians and whites with basically similar tastes-which resulted in the dispossessing of the former by a combination of political chicanery and brute force.

Disclaim Intent

We disclaim any intent to "sell" the "Red Welshmen" theory, but we feel that the shadow of the Cherokee-so strangely like his usurping brother-still lies over the land, and recently we revisited some of the Cherokee's ancient haunts.

Peck Mount and the coves it dominates, for example, is a perfect fulfillment of the Cherokee's requirements-valleys and slopes with springs, and a mountain behind for a stronghold. Some miles due north of the lookout point on Ft. Bluff, is the river front decorated with a multitude of paintings and carvings-the waterway which the Cherokee liked to have in front of him.

Between these spots, a little south of Cotaco, is an old burial ground on the Audie Huskie farm, with the deep course of a now dry spring nearby. Huskey has lived on the place for 60 years and remembers when the traces of an Indian camp could be seen there.

The tree-covered knoll there has always been called "the old Indian graveyard" we were told, but down under there were white burials, too. A straight row of foundation stones with a squared corner is exactly like the cairn type burials of early settlers, who often used the same burial mounds which the Indians had used before them.

Cherokees, we believe, also lived at the rock-ledge shelter near Gum Springs. The presence there of a drill metal-hole for grinding corn proves it was used by agricultural races long after the time of the earlier caveman hunter.

Ft. Bluff, with its high lookout point and tree grown earthworks, was used by Confederate scouts during the Civil War. But there is a tradition that this place was also the site of a last stand made by a band of Cherokees in the 1830s-the period of their eviction. Mrs. Jane Peck Gibson, whose grandfather, George W. Peck filed on the land some 10 years after the Indians had ceded it, handed the story down, as have other old timers in the region.

Impregnable Fortress

The high-piled earthworks, which may have supported a stockade, in the Cherokee style, seem to make the jutting isthmus of rock an impregnable fortress, but Mrs. Gibson told us that the Indians had a secret way of getting up and down the sheer bluffs to some rock-ledge shelters below. Last week we made an effort to find this route of descent, and did manage to get far enough down to see and photograph the rock ledges she had described. There is a fine spring down there somewhere, too, but we didn't get far enough to find it.

There are many other sites of Indian habitation in the Valley, and most of them, local archeologists say, have not yet been investigated. But just to visit these places is a thrilling experience. Whether the remote descendants of Welsh Prince Madoc ever lived here or not, innumerable generations of mysterious races did. Unanswered questions are a challenge, and the very absence of certainty gives the imagination free rein. There's always the chance that even the wildest theory might someday turn out to be true.

Indian Tomb Hollow

The site of the Battle of Indian Tomb Hollow is located about seven miles east of Moulton and approximately three miles south of Highway 36 in the Pinhook Community. The Battle of Indian Tomb Hollow, which probably occurred sometime around the 1780's, was a battle between the Chickasaws and the Creeks. The battle occurred because of a raid by Creeks into Chickasaw country and the taking of a Chickasaw maiden. The outnumbered Chickasaws finally defeated the Creeks in the Battle of Indian Tomb Hollow. Starting in 1786, the Creeks began making raids into the Chickasaw Nation because the Chickasaw Nation sided with the American government. The Creek Nation's greatest concern was the invasion of their eastern territory in Georgia by the American settlers. Creek war parties watched trails connecting the Chickasaw Nations with American settlements including those which ran through or near Lawrence County. In the spring of 1795, one-thousand Creek Warriors attacked the Chickasaw village of Long Town. Two hundred Chickasaw surprised and eventually defeated the invading Creeks (Gibson, 1971).

The Battle of Indian Tomb Hollow contains similarities to other fights which occurred during the Chickasaw-Creek War. The Chickasaws were heavily armed and well supplied by the American government. The war began after the

Chickasaws' western boundary became Caney Creek in Colbert County and after the American Revolution. During the spring of 1793, American boats delivered to the Chickasaws by way of the Ohio and Mississippi Rivers 500 stands of arms, 2,000 pounds of powder, 4,000 pounds of lead, 100 gallons of whiskey, an armory and tools (Gibson, 1971). The Chickasaw warriors were fierce fighters and have successfully challenged both DeSoto as well as the French. The Creek warriors were not as well equipped with rifles which were provided to them by the Spanish. The Chickasaws, usually outnumbered by their enemies, never lost a battle.

A huge bluff shelter in Indian Tomb Hollow

Ittaloknah: or The Battle of Indian Tomb Hollow

A story of North Alabama, Founded on the Wars of the Chickasaws
An Original Story (written expressly for *The Moulton Democrat*)
By W.H.G.
Moulton Democrat Vol. 2 November 7, 1856, No. 43

Chapter 1

One hundred years ago! What a host of thoughts flit thro' the mind with this exclamation. How varied the reminiscences of the few short years allotted to ordinary mortals; yet how much greater are those variations when the recalled days have been spanned out to months, months have flitted away into years, and the years are numbered by a century. Thoughts of the past are ever sad, but when marked by deeds of horrors or of wrongs; then they are doubly saddened. The treatment of the red man by his white oppressor has thus been marked.

In a country like ours, yet young, and constantly changing in appearances, by the rapid influx of population, and the subduing of nature, by man, the marks of years are more plainly visible, than in the older countries of earth, and in no part of our broad, extended, and beloved land, is this the fact more plainly visible, than in the northern part of noble Alabama. But a few years gone, it was a vast wilderness; its only inhabitants the wily and savage Creek, the milder but no less brave Chickasaw, the timid deer, and the savage panther.

The delineation of the Indian character has called forth some of the best talent of our country, and it may be presumed an assumption of position, in the author of this tale, to enter the arena as a delineator of their traits and characteristics. But never having met with a history of the following scenes, and trials of the Chickasaws, in their warfare with their neighbors, the Creeks; and having often visited the spots where the following scenes were enacted, and heard the incidents related by one long connected with the tribe, I have been induced to give them publicity.

It was a beautiful day in that loveliest of months, October, the deep old forest had begun to present the first indications of the approaching change of seasons. The bright scarlet hue of the sumac, the golden leaf of the sassafras, the poplar's dull yellow, contrasted beautifully, and blended agreeably with the many tints of green, of the old wood. The woodpecker, as he taps so lustily the decaying branch of yonder's ash, gives forth his shrill notes in seeming defiance to the hoarse croaking of the dark winged raven, who flits from tree to tree in yonder's copse; the gay chattering of the blithe squirrel; the shrill scream of the hawk; the rustling of undergrowth as frightened deer rushes by to evade his relentless foe; the prowling panther, but adds interest to this bright October mom, as we stand on the summit of one of the many hills now in view, and gaze upon its quiet beauty. This hill is the last of a series of undulations, that gives to the old wood to the east a wary appearance, whilst to our left, or further west, it becomes level and of a low swampy character, made so by the springs, four in number, that gush forth from the base of these hills, and empty their bright waters into the small creek bounding the western border of this flat.

How changed now the scene from that witnessed on the bright October mom in which our story opens. The bright and beautiful springs are two less in number; man in his waywardness has suffered two to become filled and lost, save in the recollections of a few. A few of the same old forest trees are here; the same old hills, the same bright sky and mellow sun, yet a mighty change has come o'er the scene. The tall lorde of the forest have fallen; the wild denizens of it have fled, and the "pale face" maketh his dwelling there. From that same old hill we now see the house of God rearing its spires to the skies; the halls of Justice; the home of the wealthy and the hovel of the poor, dot the scene with cheerfulness and sorrow at one and the same moment; whilst the hum of busy man, ever striving never satisfied, is heard in lieu of the whoop of the red man and the tread of the deer.

Often in childhood's happy hours, or boyhood's cheerful days, as I have slacked my thirst with the waters of those springs, or bathed my wearied limbs in the brook, or as I lay beneath the branches of some of those old trees, have I gazed upon the scene and wondered what would be the thoughts of one of those old warriors, who in years long- gone had drank from one of those fountains of "life giving beverage," or rested from the chase beneath the limbs of those trees, could he but awaken from his sleep, and see the great and mighty changes which had taken place since he had passed away to the spirit land.

Early on a bright October morning, eighty years, ago, our story opens. The sun had scarce marked a hand's breadth on the horizon, as two Chickasaw warriors approached the largest of the four springs we have spoken of, and leaning their rifles against the black walnut trees, from amidst whose roots the bright waters flowed, drank from the gushing fount ere proceeding to make their frugal morning meal; their simple repast consisting of a handful of parched Indian com, and a small piece of dried venison; being finished they sat for some time in perfect silence, when the elder of the two warriors arising and taking his rifle said-"The leaf of the sumac is red, and ere its fall. Ittaloknah, the pride of our tribe, must be again in the wigwam of her father. Then let us fly with the speed of the deer, for when yonder's sun shall have set and rose again, the warriors of the Chickasaws will await us in council."

With this, he started at a rapid pace from the spring, bearing north-westward in his march, followed by his companion, and again nature seemed to sleep in her solitude.

Chapter 2

That our readers may understand the expression used by the elder of the two warriors, we will have to go back from the opening of our story. The Chickasaws, a powerful and brave nation, at the time of which we write, inhabited all of the northern part of the State of Mississippi, reaching from the west tip of the Mississippi river to the meandering creek in Franklin county, Alabama, known as Caney creek. Such were the boundaries of the nation, yet claiming further east than this. The tribe was often engaged in war upon this, their claimed right. The central or more eastern counties were inhabited by the Creeks,- yet, by general consent, the middle counties of Lawrence and Morgan, were used as hunting grounds by both nations, and in truth extending further south and east, and was also the place of mortal combat on frequent occasions between them.

Some three days previous to the opening of our story, at the close of a warm sultry day, with prospect of a stormy night ahead; there sat at the door of a wigwam, situated near the eastern boundary of the Chickasaw nation, a warrior of his tribe; engaged in assisting an Indian youth in fashioning his bow. The youth seemingly fifteen years of age, stood eagerly watching his aged companion, and ever and anon addressing some question to him.

The warrior was a perfect type of his race. Remarkably tall and of perfect form for strength and endurance; he was now passed the meridian of life, and marked with the scares of many and various hard fought battles; yet that eagle eye, and those sinewy limbs, spoke forth that age had not yet quenched the fire of his youth, nor destroyed the power that had ever made him a brave of renown, and a chief of importance with his tribe. Such was Eagle Eye.

The famous marker tree in Indian Tomb Hollow

As the sun went down behind a dark and heavy mass of clouds, and the first burst of heaven's artillery was heard in the West, an aged squaw appeared at the door of the wigwam and spoke to the warrior, who now left his work, and began to gaze intently towards the East, as if eagerly watching for some one. The squaw, like the warrior, had passed the meridian of life, yet the remnants of great beauty were plainly to be seen in her features; and a close observer could, tho' dressed as an Indian, and an Indian in every action and movement, tell that the blood of the white man coursed through her veins. When an infant, captured by a party of Chickasaws from a company of French emigrants ascending the Mississippi, she alone escaped death. Taken to the Chickasaw village at Pontotac, she was then placed under the charge of an aged squaw, and being but two years of age, and reared as an Indian child, she soon forgot her parents, and grew in feelings and acts, as well as looks, a perfect Indian. She had, when about twenty years of age, blessed the wigwam of the Eagle Eye as his bride. They were the parents of but one child- a daughter- whom they called Ittaloknah or Magnolia. She, like the beautiful tree of her native mountains, possessed that grace and perfection of form and fairness of skin, that made her sobriquet perfectly appropriate.

"She left the wigwam, some hours ago with Kokomah."

The woman responded to some enquiry made of her by the warrior.

"I see someone coming" said the warrior, his attention having been called by the youth near him, to the moving of the undergrowth of the old forest, far away to the left.

"It is Pontoc," said the warrior, as an Indian youth, apparently some twelve years of age, emerged from the brush, and came running towards the group, with a countenance bespeaking alarm.

"What make Pontoc seem as the fleeing fawn, when the panther follows fast on his trail," said the old warrior to the breathless boy, who now had reached them, and stood exhausted by his fright and rapid gait. "The Creek warrior bears away the light of our wigwam; and Pontoc mourns for her he loves" spoke the youth in broken accents.

"What! my child! My Magnolia!" cried the alarmed mother seizing the boy by the arm.

"Yes, Ittaloknah is a captive. I met Kokomah, who is bleeding from his wounds, told me to haste to the wigwam of the Eagle Eye and tell the tidings while he returned to trail."

The old brave, turning to the youth we found with him when first brought before the reader said:

"Fly with the speed of the deer to the camp at Shuckanoosa and tell the warriors, that the Eaglet of my nest pants for liberty in the wigwam of the Creek: That the war cry of 'Eagle Eye' rings on the air, its warriors are wonted to sip the blood of the Creek dogs."

With a bound the youth was gone, and soon he was hidden from view by the thick copse into which he had sped. The mother stricken with grief, seemed crazed, and now her race spoke out. The warrior with all the stoic firmness of his tribe, prepared for following the trail of the Creeks. With mid-night came eight of the Chickasaw warriors from the camp at Shuckanoosa. The storm, that had been threatening all night, now broke loose in terrible fury; the winds howled in horrific strife- the rain poured in torrents- while the lightning's lurid glare, and the thunder's awful crash, but lent hideousness to the dreadful night. The nine warriors sat in the wigwam of 'Eagle Eye' in consultation.

"Let us with the coming of day follow the trail of our foes; and until then, let each one sharpen his vengeance, & prepare for the hot conflict and murderous combat," said the leading warrior of these who had obeyed the summons of 'Eagle Eye.'

He was a tall, athletic warrior, about twenty-five years of age; even more stalwart than the generality of his tribe. Altho' he yet bore the marks of many well contested battle fields. He was looked upon as the pride of the tribe, and the chosen suitor of the stolen maid.

"Does the Panther counsel waiting, when Magnolia is in the hands of the Creeks? Does he fear?" Cried the distracted mother.

"The Panther fears not the Creek; but the panther himself trails not, when the deer leaves no scent; nor does the eye of the eagle pierce this darkness. Who can follow the trail made on the water?" Said the warrior with impenetrable gravity.

"The Panther counsels caught; Kokomah will never lose sight of them and will tell us the course they fly." Said Eagle Eye.

The warriors now threw themselves upon the floor of the wigwam and were soon asleep; but with the first dawning of the mom they were up hunting the missing Indian girl. A messenger having been sent to the various portions of the nation for the braves of the tribe to meet in council in three days' time. The nine warriors pursued a South eastward course for some time, when they separated into parties of two, one however having been detailed to go back to the tribe and inform the council should the eight not return in time, to meet them at Tulumah or the four springs; agreeing among themselves to search that day, and if no signs were seen, all to return to the council leave two, who were to keep up the search until the war party from the council should reach Tulumah; and then report their success, and accompany the party in the invasion of the Creek nation.

Let us again go back to the time of Ittaloknah's leaving her parents' wigwam. Taking with her Kokomah, she went in the direction of the creek, east of the wigwam, for the purpose of fishing. Having a description of the maiden sufficient for our purpose, let us describe her companion - Kokomah, or Wild-Cat, as he was called by his tribe, was about thirty years of age, not exceeding four feet in height, with a breadth of chest and length of arm indeed remarkable. Like most of dwarfs, his features bore the appearance of greater age than really belonged to him. With all the cunning instincts of his race, he had even apparently the instincts of the animal combined with it. Taken by Eagle Eye, and by him reared, and treated with contempt by all save the inmates of this wigwam and the Panther, he seemed to hate all save these few, and for them his affections knew no bounds.

The maiden and her companion had been engaged in their occupation for some time, and as the sun was about sinking behind the mass of clouds forming in the West, they were in the act of preparing for their return home, when three Creek warriors rushed from behind some undergrowth that grew immediately in their rear, with a blow of his club, the foremost warrior felled Kokomah, and rushing past his prostrate form, seized the terrified maiden in his brawny arms, and bore her across the waters of the creek, followed by his companions, reluctantly however, as they wished to scalp Wild-Cat, but obeying the call of foremost warrior, they passed by him and were soon by the side of their leader, who, stifling the cries of the maiden, ascended the banks of the stream, and they were soon lost to view in the deep woods. Pontoc, who was near-by, hearing the cry of Magnolia, was making to her, when he was met by Kokomah, who, having revived, was hastening to the wigwam to give the alarm, but sending Pontoc, he returned, and crossing the stream, was soon on the trail of his assaulters. Coming in sight of them, he found that three more warriors had been added to their number. Darting from tree to tree, and bush to bush, and aided by the growing darkness, he was enabled to keep in sight of them without being discovered.

Pursuing their way until the storm began to break upon them, when they sought a cane near at hand, knowing that the coming of the storm would efface all signs of their trail, they would however have preferred to have kept on, but fright and fatigue had so over-come Magnolia, their march had been so rapid, they were forced on her account to stop. Wild-Cat seeking a shelter near-by, kept up his watch during the pelting of the storm, with Indian endurance. The morning broke bright and beautiful; all nature seemed gladdened by the rain storm of the passed night. As the sun was arising; the Creek warriors appeared at the opening of the cane and seemingly engaged in consultation as to the propriety of leaving their retreat, evidently fearing the signs that the now moist earth would take from their tread. After some moments thus engaged, all of them returned to the interior cane, save one, who took a position near-by to keep a watch upon the approach of any who might be in pursuit - Throughout the day Kokomah kept watch from his hiding place seemingly as immovable as the mass of stone behind which he lay concealed. Throughout the long watches of the night, he kept his place, nor left it until next morning, when with the first dawn of light, he silently withdrew further into the woods to procure water to allay his long fast, and finding upon his return some half hour later, that the cane was deserted, he set off in pursuit of the fugitives.

Moulton Democrat Vol. 2 November 14, 1856, No. 44

Chapter 3

Leaving the spring and setting out in a north-west course, as had already been said, the two warriors continued on their way with all the characteristic silence of the Indian race; but, not a bush, stick or step of ground was passed over unnoticed by them. Some hours had passed, since their leaving the spring, when reaching the banks of a large creek, crossing which and ascending the steep banks of the opposite side, when the foremost warrior suddenly stopping, and listening attentively for some seconds, said to his companion, as his acute sense of hearing detected the sound of approaching steps:

"The panther hears the tread of his enemy, and the knife of the Chickasaw must drink the blood of the Creek."

Gazing intently for some little time into the deep forest before him, he soon saw the six Creek warriors, with Magnolia bound to the wrist of one of their number, making for a crossing of the stream over which the two warriors had just crossed, some mile farther up the stream. Re-crossing the creek, the two Chickasaws made noiseless and rapid strides to reach the crossing before their enemies; reaching which, they placed themselves behind a tree, each, and patiently awaited the approach of the Creeks. Possessing each a rifle, whilst the party of Creeks had only one fire arm, the remainder being armed with bows, they hoped to soon make the two parties more nearly equal in number, when the silent; but no less fatal knife must decide the fate of the day. Directing his companion to select one of the Creek warriors for his victim, the Panther chose as his, the one bearing the rifle. Rapidly approaching the spot where the two warriors lay concealed, the Creeks were soon within reach of their aim, and simultaneously they both fired, and with a bound two of the Creek warriors "bit the dust." Darting instantly to some covert, the remaining Creeks prepared for battle, and now began that mode of attack incident to Indian warfare. Darting from tree to tree, from bush to bush, and even sometimes crawling upon the earth to procure an advantageous position. A Creek warrior in passing thus from a tree to a bush nearby, so as to place the Chickasaw within range of his bow, received Tullah's fire, and like his two companions, fell a corpse. The Chickasaw brave, elated by his success, exposing a portion of his body, received the contents of the rifle dropped by the Creek, slain by the Panther, but which had been gained by a Creek warrior, and with a yell fell lifeless to the earth; and again the sharp crack of the Panther's rifle rings upon the air, and another Creek falls. Reloading his rifle, and eagerly and intently watching for one of the two remaining warriors, the Panther did not hear the approach of his enemy in his rear. One of the Creek braves had managed in the confusion of the attack, to reach, unperceived the extreme left of the Panther; and throwing himself upon the ground, had with serpent's speed and stillness, reached a tree immediately in the rear of the Chickasaw, near enough to reach him with a bound. Slowly, but cautiously he raised himself erect, and with the spring of a wild panther, he pinioned his arms around those of his adversary; the remaining Creek warrior being aware of the intention of his companion, was, with a few bounds, by his side, and in the best of time; for the Panther having freed his arm, and knife in hand, was in the act of piercing his assailant through; but the Creek warrior seized the raised arm of the Panther. He was now bound and led captive to the spot where Magnolia had been confined at the onset of the attack.

173

"The nuptials of Topeka shall be lighted by the fire which burns the Chickasaw warrior," said the Creek warrior, who led the Panther to the place where Magnolia sat.

"The Panther's knife has drank deep of the blood of the Creeks; and his wigwam is decked with their scalps. The Chickasaw knows how to die and he fears not the fire of the Creek sacrifice," was the Panther's reply.

Securing their prisoners firmly, they proceeded to collect the bodies of their fallen companions, in a sunken place nearby; and knowing now that pursuit was being made, they set out at a rapid gate for their lodges with their prisoners.

Let us return to Kokomah, whom we left on the trail of Magnolia and her captives. He found but little difficulty in following the trail, which left the cave and passed eastward and near where he had been concealed during his watch. Not long on their trail he came to a spot, where from the eminence of a hill he saw in the distance two of the Creek warriors further to the left, disappear in the depths of the forest; leaving the main trail he struck across the country to the point where he had seen them disappear, thus saving some time as well as walking. Reaching this point he struck the trail left by the two Indians, but did not follow it more than a mile, until becoming convinced that none save the two warriors he had seen had passed along there, he returned to the eminence we have seen him leave, and again taking the main trail leading southeast, he followed it slowly, for the Creeks had taken every precaution to obliterate any signs that could lead in their pursuit. Following it for some three or four miles, and reaching a small stream which the trail crossed, he now found for the first time some sign of Magnolia being with this portion of the Creeks, and was now convinced that the two warriors had left the main party as a 'ruse' and would again join them.

He found here the print of a human finger, the print had been made by placing the finger while wet and stained with mud upon the leaf of a bush upon the side of the trail. With a suppressed cry of joy he began again to follow the trail with renewed vigor. The mark was made with earth of a different color from any in the vicinity of this spot; and he felt assured Magnolia, whilst in the cave, had secured the earth with which the mark had been made, and which evidently escaped the notice of the captors; for Wild-Cat had seen plainly that unusual pains had been taken to evade the vengeance of the Chickasaws. Following the trail rapidly, (he had some hours left the spot where he had found the mark by Ittaloknah,) when he caught the sound of fire arms at a great distance; hurrying his already rapid steps, he reached an eminence that overlooked the combat we have described between the two Chickasaw braves and the Creeks; as the last fire of the Panther's rifle felled the Creek warrior. Seeing the Creek who was approaching the rear of the Panther, and adopting a similar mode of approach, he crawled as fast as the uneven nature of the ground over which he was compelled to pass would permit; hoping to intercept the Creek in his course; he had not however, passed over more than half of the distance, when he heard the cry of the Creek warrior as he fastened upon the Panther, and seeing the second warrior approaching to the aid of his companion, he well knew ere he could reach the combatants, the struggle would be over, he changed his direction and now made for the spot from which he had seen the warrior advance, when he began to prepare for his attack upon the Chickasaw, supposing that their captive was confined there. To succeed in this and avoid detection, he was forced to retrace his course some distance and then make a considerable detour. He had made the return and was fast hastening towards the spot where Magnolia sat, when he saw the two Creek warriors advancing with their prisoner, it was with sorrow that he saw them place their prisoners near them while engaged in securing the bodies of their fallen companions. When again they set out on their journey he was on their trail, determining with the darkness of night to liberate his friends.

Chapter 4

Pursuing their course still southeast, they did not stop with the fall of night, but continued on their way, until long uninterrupted march overcame with fatigue, Magnolia; and they were reluctantly forced to stop. It was near midnight when they halted; the place chosen for their rest was in a small gorge or hollow of the mountain, where firmly securing their prisoners, the two warriors made preparations for their night watch. The Creek who had addressed himself to the Panther upon his capture, and who was the leader of the party, took first watch, whilst the other slept at the feet of the prisoners; Topeka sat reclining against a tree near their heads. The spot where they rested was level and clear of all undergrowth, for several places around, save the side on which Topeka sat. A space in the rear of the tree against which he leaned; the rank grass and undergrowth held perfect sway, covering the earth with a dense carpet and shelter.

Soon after the party had assumed their various positions, the stilly calmness of the night was broken by the hideous scream of that terror of the red man-the panther; for there seems to have been a superstitious horror on the part of the southern tribes of Indians towards this ferocious beast. Starting from their positions, the two Creek warriors seized their rifles; for with the fall of the Chickasaw brave, and the capture of the Panther, they had appropriated their rifles to their own use; awaited a nearer approach of the animal. But very soon they heard its shrill scream farther down the gorge, as if being frightened, he had left the spot where first heard. With the first cry, the two prisoners started, but with the last the Panther spoke something to his companion in the Chickasaw language.

All was again hushed in death-like silence, and the Creeks had resumed the places from which they had been startled. But let us return to Wild-Cat. So soon as he saw the party stop, he approached near enough to see the positions the various ones of the group had taken. Having done so he again fell back farther from them, imitating the cry of the panther, he hastily passed farther down the gorge hoping thus to allay any suspicions that might have arisen in the minds of the Creeks, should they have heard the noise made by the breaking of a dry stick upon which he had inadvertently trod, and also arrest the attention of the Chickasaw; for he well knew this was a favorite signal with the captive warrior; which was attended with complete success, as we have seen. Stealthily approaching the camp, with his knife in his mouth, and nearing it he threw himself upon the ground and began by slow and well-guarded movements, to approach the rear of the tree against which Topeka leaned. He had reached a point within a few feet of the tree against which the warrior reclined, when Topeka sprang to his feet, and gazed intently in the direction of the spot where the dwarf lay concealed in the high grass; but neither seeing or hearing anything further to excite his suspicion, he again sat reclining against the tree. Once more he slept - for worn out by long and arduous traveling and feeling secure- HE SLEPT! Fatal security! Kokomah, by slow and noiseless movements neared the tree. Reaching which, he seized his knife in his hand, and in a moment more it was buried in the heart of Topeka; and with his long and sinewy arm, bore him gently to the earth, as if he sank in gentle sleep; without showing any of his body to the other Creek warrior, who hearing the deep groan of Topeka, had raised himself to a sitting posture, but seeing his companion sinking gradually to the' earth, supposed he was overcome with sleep, had stretched himself upon the earth, and following the example of his chief, he soon again slept. With the same serpent-like motion, Kokomah approached the captives, and with his knife severed the bonds that bound the Panther's hands. The Chickasaw warrior had been able to see Wild-Cat as he passed over the slain body of Topeka, and was prepared for release. Wild-Cat had possessed himself of Topeka's knife as he crossed his body, and placing this in the Panther's hand, with a bound he reached the spot where lay the remaining Creek. But the warrior had been awakened by the preparation for the bound, and was on his feet in a moment to receive his assailant; seizing each other in mortal embrace, they fell to the ground. The Panther severing the bonds that held his feet confined, rushed into the combat; calling to Wild-Cat; to ascertain his position, and finding him beneath, with his arms pinioned around the Creek warrior, who was striving manfully to relieve one arm, but in vain, the knife of the Panther soon, put an end to the combat. Relieving Magnolia, upon consultation they determined to remain in their present position until day. The two Chickasaws now took their post of watch, while the Indian maiden slept.

Moulton Democrat Vol. 2 November 21, 1856, No. 45

Chapter 5

With the first rays of light the Chickasaws were on their way back to their nation; and with what difference in feelings, from those experienced on the previous night as they passed over the same trail they were now retracing! Leaving the mountains, they now entered the beautiful valley of land running across the now county of Lawrence in Alabama. When the sun was some two or three hours above the horizon, they met, near Tulamah a party of Chickasaws under the lead of Eagle Eye, who were fast following the trail made by the Creeks and their prisoners, the night previous.

At the meeting of the council, two of the party of the returned warriors, who had set out in search of the captive, reported that in crossing the Okhomah or Town Creek, they had passed the place of the battle, as we have described, and also found the bodies of the four Creeks, and likewise that of Tullmah. They well knew that the Panther was a captive, or he would have met them in Council; they also feared for Wild-Cat, who was now missing since the capture of Magnolia.

The meeting was indeed a joyous one; and as neither party had as yet made their morning meat, they were in the act of going to a small spring nearby, when with a whoop of a set of fiends, a party of Creeks fired upon them from the surrounding trees and brush.

Above: A marker tree in Indian Tomb Hollow.

A party of Creeks, some sixty in number, being out in search of the six warriors, whom we have seen slain, and finding the bodies of Topeka and his companion, had followed the trail of the returning Chickasaws, and had succeeded in making a near approach to the party, unperceived; so much were they engaged with the returned captives. Darting to some covert, the Chickasaws began to battle for life. With the first fire, several of their number having fallen, and the assailing party being more numerous, the odds were greatly against them. Three of the Creek warriors seeing Magnolia, and knowing her to be the cause of the loss of their braves, determined upon her recapture. Gradually advancing to her rear, which reaching, they rushed upon her, one seizing her in his arms, bore her shrieking for aid, farther into that part of the woods occupied by his party; her cry caused her friends to rush to her rescue and in so doing, exposed themselves to the fire of their enemy. This so much weakened their force, that they were compelled to retire, leaving Magnolia again a captive in the hands of their foemen. Returning, towards evening, from the pursuit, they buried their few slain, and scalped their slain enemies, proceeded with their captive homeward.

The retiring Chickasaws, collecting their forces found that they had lost twenty of their number. Upon consultation, knowing that the Creeks had withdrawn, they determined to camp for the night, and await a large party of warriors who had not reached the council in time to set out with them, and sending one of their number on to hasten their advance, they proceeded to camp. They had not however, long concluded upon their course of action, when they saw coming towards them, the expected aid. Returning to the battle field they had but little trouble in finding the trail of the Creek warriors, following which, with the utmost speed, they soon found a spot where their enemy had halted to make their mid-day meal, or rather what should have been their mid-day repast, hoping thereby to be enabled to march during a portion of the night, fearing a pursuit by the friends of the maiden. It was evident that they had not left this spot a great while. Towards sun set, the Panther and Kokomah, who were in the lead, caught a glimpse of the Creek party, and saw that the fatigue of Magnolia, whom the Creeks were actually bearing along, would force the party to halt for a night's rest.' They saw them pass around a spur of the mountain, which they had reached, and enter a gorge or hollow. Following to this point, the two Chickasaws saw the disposition of their foes. Returning now to their friends, and reporting their success, they hastily set forward to avenge the defeat of the morning.

The place which the Creeks had chosen for their hiding place was a large natural amphitheater. Entering it from the north, the sides rose quite abruptly, and gradually enlarging from the mouth, where it was about fifty paces in width for some distance, when having reached the width of two hundred paces, it gradually closed again, and ended in a perpendicular ledge of rock some forty feet in height, over which passed a stream of limpid water. Some six or eight feet from the base of this ledge rock, on one side it shelved off into a cave of considerable length but shallow. The Chickasaw warriors now approached the point around which the Creeks had passed and disposing their forces so as to open a deadly fire upon the unsuspecting Creeks. This was soon done, and pouring a well-aimed fire of rifle balls and arrows upon them, with a whoop rushed upon their astonished enemies. Soon however they returned the fire and each sought some shelter. The Panther and Kokomah side by side, approached the spot where they supposed Magnolia lay bound, and as they neared it, two of the Creek warriors, perceiving their design, rushed forward to meet them. The Panther singled out his adversary, and knife in hand they advanced to mortal combat, and were soon engaged in deadly strife. Seizing each other they fell to the earth; but the Creek warrior was uppermost; disengaging his arm, he was in the act of pinning the Chickasaw brave to the ground, when a blow from Kokomah's club felled him, and the knife soon came reeking from his heart. Wild-Cat had in the conflict possessed himself of a tomahawk, and as he advanced to meet his foe, sent it with unerring aim, which staggering him, gave the Chickasaw the advantage, and in a moment more the fatal knife finished the work. Kokomah now proceeded to the aid of Panther, and we have seen how very opportunely.

Detaching six warriors with rifles, Eagle Eye ordered them to the top of the ledge of rock, towards which the Creeks were retiring slowly, leaving the hollow they rapidly marched to the designated point, where they held the Creek warriors at their mercy; attacked in front and rear, they were fast falling beneath the murderous fire of their enemy. Their number now reduced to twenty warriors, who seeing no chance for escape save in a desperate assault upon these in front; thus opening a way for some to fly. With a simultaneous movement they rushed their foe, and the combat now became truly terrific. Eagle Eye was in the direct course of the principal part of the Creek warriors, and received and sustained alone for some time the entire shock. Firing his rifle as they advanced, one fell a corpse; seizing his rifle as a club, he felled two more to the earth, now throwing his rifle away, the combat becoming too close to use it longer, he seized his knife, and with unerring aim, sent it deep into the chest of one of the advancing Creeks; darting aside to avoid the descending knife of a Creek brave, he sent his fatal knife into the vitals of another foeman. A powerful Creek rushing upon him, closed in a hand to hand strife. The Creek bore Eagle Eye to the ground, where they struggled hard for the advantage; the contest thickened around them; in truth, the infuriated combatants so retarded the actions of Eagle Eye and his assailant, as to greatly prolong the contest. But the age and superhuman exertions of the Chickasaw Chief began to tell, and soon the knife of the Creek drank the blood of the brave old warrior. Arising from his slain foe, and brandishing his reeking blade high overhead, gave a shout of defiance, but it was his last slain- his last war hoop;- the knife of the Panther, who had been striving to reach Eagle Eye, but too late, entered his throat and he fell lifeless to the earth.

The fight was fast drawing to a close; there now remained only ten Creek warriors to combat, not now for victory, or even life, but to die with as many slain around them as possible; these few were fast falling beneath the Chickasaw knives, for this now was the only instrument of death used by either party. Five of that ten now lay weltering in their own gore; the remaining number, seizing upon a favorable moment, when a gap was left in the ranks of the Chickasaws, rushed for it, and bearing beneath them the only warrior in their course, made for the mouth of the gorge, followed by the entire band of now victorious Chickasaws, who with a yell of maddened they rushed forward in pursuit.

The Creeks, two wounded, the others exhausted by the unequal contest, were fast nearing the mouth of the gorge; but with the Chickasaws at their heels, led by Panther, and who were gaining upon them, already one of the wounded Creeks is beneath his fatal blade, in another moment it sinks deep in the quivering flesh of the poor Indian. The other wounded Creek has fallen, and the three remaining ones were destined to soon follow their slain companions, when a shriek was heard, coming from the gorge, which they now had left. All knew it to be Magnolia, who cried for help. Instantly the larger part of the Chickasaws hastened back to the gorge. This diversion in their favor, enabled the flying Creeks to make good their escape.

Let us return to the hollow. Magnolia upon the onset of the battle was led into the cave at the head of the gorge, where, unconfined, she was a witness to the terrible conflict. She saw the onslaught of the Creeks upon her father, and also saw him fall; but as the combat thickened around him; she was unable to tell whether he had arisen, and was yet leading the now victorious Chickasaws, or lay a corpse amidst the heap of slain, she saw around the spot where he had fallen. The battle fast receding down the gorge, she determined to allay her anxiety by going to the spot where she had seen her father fall; reaching which, she beheld his lifeless body, with his life- blood clotting the grass at her feet;- with a wild shriek she cast herself upon the inanimate clay. Twas this that called back the Chickasaw warriors; but another heard it and it was the last cry of the Indian maiden. A Creek warrior, stunned by a blow from her father's rifle, recovering from it, and hearing the battle passing away, was arising from the ground to make good his escape and hearing the cry of the maiden, and seeing who it was, determined, with a fiendish purpose, to be yet avenged for the loss of his companions. Magnolia falling upon the corpse of her father prevented her being aware of the approach of the fiend. Seeing no one near he determined to bear her away captive, seizing her and stifling her cries with his hand, bore her away to the east side of the gorge where it was easy of ascent, knowing that if he could reach the top of the ledge of rock; he could soon, by reaching a creek, evade the search of Chickasaws.

He was fast nearing the place of ascent; Magnolia seeing her friends returning, and fearing they would not see her captor, made a desperate effort to free herself from his grasp, and although unsuccessful, served to draw the attention of her friends to her. With the bound of a deer, the Panther sped to her relief. The Creek encumbered by his burden, saw he must fall a prey to his rapidly advancing foe; with a fiendish yell, he raised his knife high above his head, and buried to the hilt in the bosom of the Indian maiden; and with quivering limbs she sank from the embrace of her murderer. The Panther saw the hellish deed, and it lent speed to his already rapid steps; and ere he reached the summit of the hill, the death of Magnolia was revenged by the knife of her lover.

Returning to Magnolia, who yet lived, but was fast sinking into death, he heard from her, why she screamed, and the attack of her murderer.

"Bury me with my father, down in the gorge there, where my lovely namesake will bloom in spring time o'er my grave, and where the spirit of Magnolia may wander in the bright light of the summer morn;" said the dying maiden.

A few minutes more and her spirit was with her father's, in the happy "hunting ground" of the red man. The Panther now bore her body to the place where her father's lay. The returning warriors, grief-stricken with the loss of

Eagle Eye and his lovely child, prepared in solemn silence to perform the last sad rites to the dead. A place, just out of the cave, at the head of the gorge, was prepared for the bodies of the old warrior and his daughter. Covered with cane wicker work, by the light of the pale moon, and with death-like stillness, their bodies, with the old warrior's arms, were placed in their narrow bed, and covered with a massive stone; they were left in the solitude that pervaded that gloomy dell-the soothing sounds of the falling waters alone breaking the silence; seemed as a lullaby to the moldering bones of Eagle Eye and his child.

The bodies of the fallen Chickasaws were placed within the cave, and covered with stones-the enemies scalped;-the victorious but grieved Chickasaws set out for their nation, and home of the bereaved wife and mother; the now doubly bereaved "White Lily." The moon looked down upon the still and unbroken silence that reigned where, but a short time before, the wild whoop, the fatal rifle crack, the death groans and harsh words of infuriated man held sway.

The white man ere long began to be seen in the country, and the red man was fast failing before him. In autumn's sad time of each year, for a long while, an Indian might be seen wending his way to "Indian Tomb Hollow." Grief had marked his sad features and wan countenance. With the taciturnity of his race he bore them without a murmur, and when at length he felt his days numbered, he wended his way to the spot of all others most dear to him, and there upon the grave of her he had loved so well in life, he breathed his last. The "pale face" now soon occupied the land far and near; not satisfied with his treatment to the red man, during life, his bones were not sacred in death. The grave of Eagle Eye and Magnolia was tom open, and their bodies were left to molder in the winds of winter and the dews of summer.

Note: It was with sorrow I saw the bones of the red man and his child tom from their resting place, to deck the mansion of a would-be gentleman. When last I visited the spot, (9 miles south east of Moulton,) nature had, as if in honor of her who slept there, purposely decked the "hollow" with the White Magnolia, with its long pendant leaves and snowy bloom; it seemed to mourn and yet pay tribute to the memory of the pride of the Chickasaws.

The burial of the bones in the "sink," as related in the first battle, gave grounds for a strange accusation of murder, against a younger brother by an elder one, and but for the testimony of an old resident, might have terminated badly to the accused.

[THE END]

This battle took place near the town of Moulton, in a field some two hundred yards north west of the residence formerly occupied by J.M. Jackson, Esq. When a boy, I have picked up arrowheads, and on one occasion found an Indian bone with the stone arrow head still in it. At the first settling of this town, bones were plentifully scattered over this spot.

Rob Cox stands in the High Town Path that crosses the upper drainage of Indian Tomb Hollow.

Oakville of the Warrior Mountains

Oakville Indian Mounds Park & Museum

The Oakville Indian Mounds Museum was designed on the basis of the Cherokee Capitol at the village of Chota. In addition, a council house at Cowe was described by William Bartram. These two descriptions were utilized in the construction of the Oakville Museum.

Timberlake Describes Chota Townhouse

The Cherokee Council house was described by Lt. Henry Timberlake, in 1761, at the Cherokee capitol of Chota on The Little Tennessee River. Chota was one of the most important Overhill towns of the Cherokee nation, and was the site of the national heptagon council house.

The present day site of Chota is now inundated by the waters of Tellico Lake. The Chota town site was located just a, short distance from the base of Chilhowee Dam in East Tennessee near Vonore, Tennessee. Some of the remains of Cherokee Indians were moved to the Sequoyah Birthplace Museum just some two miles north of Vonore on the banks of Tellico Lake. Just one mile east of the Sequoyah Museum is the reconstructed Fort Loudoun.

Chota was the major political center and capitol of the Cherokee Nation during the middle 1700's. The political system, social life, and religious ceremonies were centered around the Townhouse, The Summer Pavilion, and Grand Plaza. From the following text found in *Tellico Archaeology* by Jefferson Chapman printed in 1985, Lt. Henry Timberlake describes the townhouse at Chota in 1761- 1762 as follows:

"The town-house, in which are *transacted all public business and diversions, is raised with wood, and covered over with earth, and has all the appearance of a small mountain at a little distance. It is built in the form of a sugar loaf, and large enough to contain 500 persons, but extremely dark, having, besides the door, which is narrow that but one at a time can pass, and that after much winding and turning, but one small aperture to let the smoke out, which is so ill contrived, that most of it settles in the ancient amphitheater, the seats being raised one above another, leaving an area in the middle, in the center of which stands the fire; the seats of the head warriors are nearest it.*

The townhouse at Chota was first constructed with four central support posts. A short time later, the structure was expanded to the form observed by Timberlake, employing eight central support posts and measuring 60 feet in diameter. A myriad of post holes within the townhouse perimeter once contained the structural supports for benches in the two townhouses. To the east of the townhouse were found over 70 large refuse-filled pits; archaeologists interpret these pits as originally source areas for the soil that covered the roof of the structure. A corridor of postholes at the south side marked the townhouse entrance. Opposite the townhouse entrance was a summer townhouse or pavilion. This structure measured 48 by 23 feet. A less substantial structure the pavilion was probably a roofed, open shed that contained benches. Beyond the pavilion was the plaza which was bordered by domestic dwellings and the edge of the river terrace. Timberlake observed banners flown from the townhouse and from poles on the plaza; archaeological evidence for these was not found. Townhouses were also discovered in excavations at Toqua, Tomotley, and Mialoquo."

William Bartram's Description of the Cherokee Council House

During the late 1700's, William Bartram, an English naturalist, traveled extensively throughout the southeastern U.S. As published in his 1791 book titled *Travels of William Bartram*, the following is a description of Cherokee dwellings at Cowe:

"The town of Cowe consists of about one hundred dwellings, near the banks of the Tanase, on both sides of the river. The Cherokees construct their habitations on a different plan from the Creeks; that is, but one oblong four square building, of one story high; the materials consisting of logs or trunks of trees, stripped of their bark, notched at their ends, fixed one upon another, and afterwards plastered well, both inside and out, with clay well-tempered with dry grass, and the whole covered or roofed with the bark of the chestnut tree or long broad shingles.

This building is however partitioned transversely, forming three apartments, which communicate with each other by inside doors; each house or habitation has besides a little conical house, covered with dirt, which is called the winter or hot-house; this stands a few yards distant from the mansion-house, opposite the front door. Bartram also described in detail the council house which is given in the following paragraphs.

The councilor town-house is a large rotunda, capable of accommodating several hundred people; it stands on the top of an ancient artificial mount of earth, of about twenty feet perpendicular, and the rotunda on the top of it being above thirty feet more, gives the whole fabric an elevation of about sixty feet from the common surface of the ground. But it may be proper to observe, that this mount, on which the rotunda stands, is of a much ancient date than the building, and perhaps was raised for another purpose. The Cherokees themselves are as ignorant as we are, by what people or for what purpose these artificial hills were raised...

The rotunda is constructed after the following manner: they first fix in the ground a circular ring of posts or trunks of trees, about six feet high, at equal distances, which are notched at the top, to receive into them, from one to another, a range of beams or wall plates; within this is another circular order of very large and strong pillars, above twelve feet high, notched in like manner at top, to receive another range of wall plates; and within this is yet another or third range of stronger and higher pillars but fewer in number, and standing at a greater distance from each other; and lastly, in the center stands a very strong pillar, which forms the pinnacle of the building, and to which the rafters center at top; these rafters are strengthened and bound together by cross beams and laths, which sustain the roof or covering, which is a layer of bark neatly placed, and tight enough to exclude the rain, and sometimes they cast a thin superficial of earth over all.

There is but one large door, which serves at the same time to admit light from without and the smoke to escape when a fire is kindled; but as there is but a small fire kept, sufficient to give light at night, and that fed with dry small sound wood divested of its bark, there is but little smoke. All around the inside of the building, betwixt the second range of pillars and the wall, is a range of cabins or sophas, consisting of two or three steps, one above or behind the other, in theatrical order, where the assembly sit or lean down; these sophas are covered with mats or carpets, very curiously made of thin splints of Ash or Oak, woven or platted together;' near the great pillar in the center the fire is kindled for light, near which the musicians seat themselves, and round about this the performers exhibit their dances and other shows et public festivals, which happen almost every night throughout the year.

The Oakville Museum Building

The seven-sided Oakville Indian Mounds Museum is a modified design of a Cherokee council house based on the descriptions of Lt. Henry Timberlake and William Bartram. The seven sides are representative of the sacred Cherokee number seven. The Cherokee had seven clans or family units which were maternal or based on the mother's blood line. The seven clans were the Bird, Deer, Wolf, Long Hair (Twister), Wild Potato, Red Paint, and Blue (Panther). It was illegal for a member of one clan to marry another person from the same clan. Each family unit would assemble in the council house on a set of bleachers designated for their clan.

The Oakville Indian Mound Museum

The Cherokee style of government consisted of a dual form: Red officials represented war and were elected by popular vote based on the bravery; white officials represented peace and were inherited with the son of the chief's oldest sister being in line as a white principal official. According to *The Cherokee People* by Thomas E. Mails, and printed in 1992, the following represented the white organization:

The principal officers in the white, or peace, *organization* were *as follows, with categories one through five and ten being members of the priestly cast:*

1. The chief of the tribe, or Great High Priest, who is variously called Uku, Ookah, and other ceremonial titles.

188

2. Ulo tv, the chief's principal assistant, also called "right-hand man" or "the one who fanned him."

3. Ti nv li no he ski, the seven counselors who represented the seven clans.

4. A tsi nv sti, the chief's messenger.

5. Ti kv no tsi li ski, the chief speaker.

6. The council of elder, or beloved, men.

7. The Beloved, or Pretty, or War, Women.

8. A ke yv gv sta, the women who warmed water to wash the chief

9. Lesser officers required for specific ceremonies included: seven hunters, seven cooks, seven overseers, seven fire makers, seven cleansers, musicians, attendants at the Ookah dance, and Yo wah hymn singer.

10. Nv no hi ta hi, the priest who superintended the building of the hothouse.

The above officials served in the national capital and as officials for the entire tribe. But with the exception of those listed in category nine, since most of the ceremonies requiring these were held at the national heptagon, in each of the larger towns of the tribe the same series of officials were repeated."

Seven was also the number of directions of the Cherokee and were as follows: North, East, South, West, up, down, and within the person. North was represented by the color blue. East was represented by the color red. South was represented by the color white. West was represented by the color black.

Two important directions were East and West. East represented the light, the beginning of the day, dawn, beginning of life, the spring of the year, and birth. West represented darkness, the end of the day, night, fall of the year, ending of life, and death. Blue represented failure, disappointment, or unsatisfied desire. White represented peace and happiness. Seven also indicates completion, the full circle.

In addition, the Oakville Museum contains a seven foot wooden statue of Sequoyah carved from a five foot diameter white oak tree. Sequoyah was born in 1776 at Tuskegee Village just outside the gates of Fort Loudoun on the banks of the Little Tennessee River. Fort Loudoun was the first British fort built in the Overhill Towns. Sequoyah was thought to be the son of Nathaniel Guess (or Gist) and Wurteh.

This large statue of Sequoyah by master carver David V. Goodlett took two years to complete

Sequoyah Statue

Sequoyah is the only man in history to single handed develop an alphabet so his people could read and write in their own language. Sequoyah was a mixed blood Cherokee with white and Indian ancestry. Sequoyah's father was Nathaniel Gist, who became an officer in the colonial army. His mother, Wurteh, was a sister to Cherokee Chief Doublehead, who controlled the Lawrence County area from 1790 to his death in the summer of 1807.

As a young boy, Sequoyah, known as George, was in Dekalb County, Alabama. Sequoyah helped negotiate the 1816 Turkey Town Treaty which gave up Cherokee claims to Lawrence County. In 1818, he moved to Arkansas where he completed the Cherokee alphabet.

His need and curiosity with writing prompted a desire to help educate his people with a written Cherokee language. Sequoyah's name has been immortalized in a national park, a tree, a nuclear power plant, and a museum. Sequoyah died in Mexico in 1843 while searching for lost Cherokees.

Oakville Ceremonial Woodland Mound

The ceremonial mound covers about 1.8 acres, stands 27 feet high, and is considered to be at least 2,000 years old. The only known modifications to the mound were from cutting a lower portion of the sides to provide more area for farming. In addition, the top of the mound has been repeatedly plowed which has caused the top edge of the mound to get steeper and probably flatter. The steps to the top of the mound were placed in an old road to the top of the mound.

The ceremonial mound has never been excavated but was visited by a team of Smithsonian archaeologists in 1924. During their site visit three additional smaller mounds were identified as being in close proximity to the large ceremonial mound. In addition, the Smithsonian team reported of another mound with a modern cemetery ¼ mile to the north which is the Copena burial mound.

Another mound with a modern cemetery was noted as being two miles to the Southwest. The Smithsonian archaeologists were doing the survey of the

Wilson Dam Reservoir prior to its impoundment. They reported that the three small mounds were in the process of being plowed down.

The Copena Mound at Oakville

Oakville Copena Mound

The Copena people lived during the Woodland Period from 1,000 B.C. to 1,000 A.D. Their society did not extend much farther south than the Warrior Mountains which can be seen to the south of the Ceremonial Mound. The Copena Society did not extend a great distance north of the Hogohegee (Tennessee) River. They were noted for their use of copper and galena objects. They were great traders in conch shells, marble, greenstone, copper, and galena objects.

The Copena was agrarian people who depended heavily on the crops of corn, pumpkins, beans, and other vegetable products as their primary food supply. Their practice of mound burial along with other burial rituals distinguishes this group. In a cave near Coffee Slough on the Tennessee River near Florence, an important Copena leader was buried beneath a flow stone in the cave. His body had been sealed within a putty mixture of clay, ash, and crushed mussel shells. This type of burial was common for the Copena people.

The Copena Mound at Oakville is one of the largest burial mounds in North Alabama which is still in good condition. The mound was utilized for the burial of Copena Indian people. The mounds were made by one basket full of dirt at a time. Stone spades were used to dig the soil from borrow pits with the soil transferred by baskets to the mound site. The probable borrow pit was the depression that now contains Oakville Pond, the body of water northeast of the Ceremonial Mound.

Other Local Mounds

In addition to the five mounds at Oakville, other Indian mounds are found scattered throughout the area. During the Smithsonian visit, archaeologists were in the process of excavating the Alexander Mound some four miles Southwest of Oakville just up West Flint Creek and another mound some three miles Southwest from Oakville on Pope Warren's property. The Alexander Mound and Warren Mound were practically completely excavated. The Alexander Mound is about two miles south of Highway 36 with the Warren Mound about one quarter mile south of Highway 36.

The McMillian Mound was located about three miles directly south of the Ceremonial Mound on Emmitt McMillian's property. The McMillian Mound was graded down by Howell Smith and contained large chunks of galena and many other artifacts.

About five miles southeast of the Ceremonial Mound, a long a ridge within sight of an easterly facing bluff line of Sand Mountain contained much evidence of long term occupation. The remains of the five mounds can still be seen. Sand Mountain mounds are near the northeastern edge of the public lands of Bankhead National Forest. In the Oakville Museum, a parakeet effigy pipe in the large wall hanging collection came from one of the Sand Mountain Mounds. Just east of the Sand Mountain Mounds were three additional mounds that have been destroyed.

Several other smaller mounds were located within close proximity to the Oakville Ceremonial Mound but have long since been destroyed. The close proximity of the many outlying mounds lends credibility to the probability of Oakville being the religious and social center of the Copena Indian Society.

Black Warriors' Path

Along the western edge of the Ceremonial Mound is the Black Warriors' Path or Mitchell Trace. The path was a major trading route utilized by Indian people. The path connected Fort Hampton near the Tennessee River crossing at Elk (Chuwalee) River Shoals to Fort Mitchell near the Chattahoochee River in present day Russell County, Alabama.

The Black Warriors' Path is clearly shown on the 1818 Melish map shows the path crossing both the West Fork of Flint Creek and Elam Creek. These crossings are still clearly visible just one mile north of the burial mound.

Remnants of the very old road are still visible on the west side of the ceremonial Indian mound at Oakville. In addition, just south of Lindsey Cemetery, the old road bed is clearly visible as it crosses U.S. Forest Service property into Beaty Hollow and on into Poplar Log Cove.

Indian Removal along the Black Warriors' Path

Fort Mitchell, which marked the southern-most point of the Mitchell Trace (Black Warriors' Path) that passed through the Oakville Indian Mounds Park, played a vital role in the final days of the Creek Indian removal during the 1830's. By 1835, many Creeks had been removed west. A detachment of 511 Creeks passed through the Oakville Indian Mounds Park along the Mitchell Trace on December 19, 1835.

The Old Mitchell Trace crosses the West fork of Flint Creek approximately one mile north of the Oakville Indian Mounds Park. After crossing the Fish Dam Ford on West Flint, the old wagon road turns west toward Moulton. It was probably along this route the Creek Indian people traveled on the Moulton arriving there on December 19, 1835. Remnants of the old road to Moulton can be observed on County Road 186 approximately one- half of a mile south of Elam Creek. Again, the old road is visible where it crosses the Drag Strip Road on County Road 184 just one -fourth mile south of Elam Creek. The old road continues west toward Moulton crossing the old Pinhook Road, and enters Moulton near the Byler Road and Pinhook Road junction.

Town of Oakville

Oakville was the first of four towns established in Lawrence County, Alabama around 1820. Very quickly, Oakville became the political focal point in southeast Lawrence County. Prominent people moved to Oakville and included three doctor's families- Dr. Tandy W. Walker; Dr. Fleming Hodges; and Dr. James Key. Each of these doctors has family members buried in the Indian burial mound within the Oakville Indian Mounds Park. Other settlers buried in the mound include military officers and their families.

All the early settlers buried in the Copena Mound were apparently well to do for their time. Nearly all of the Oakville settler burials had false stone crypts place on their graves. The methods of burial included placing field stones and rocks on top of the bodies to prevent wild animals from digging up the graves. The false stone crypts were cut using hand held star drills. The corners of some of metal links fastened in corner holes. The capstone held the metal links in place.

Oakville had a large spring which supplied water to the town. The spring ran toward the northwest for approximately one half mile until it ran into a limestone crevasse. In 1817, when the first surveyors crossed into the 16th section near the park's fishing pier, they noted the limestone crevasse where the water from the spring run underground.

After settlement of the area, a hog pen was eventually built around the crevasse. The crevasse stopped up and the water flooded toward the town of Oakville. Soon after, the back water created Oakville Pond. The spring water became contaminated causing the people to come down with the bloody flux, a severe form of dysentery. Shortly after 1860, the Town of Oakville was abandoned.

Below: The Black Warrior's Path as it crosses Fish Dam Ford on Flint Creek, just north of Oakville Museum.

SOURCES

Brown, Virginia Pounds and Laurella Owens, <u>The World of the Southern Indians</u>. Birmingham: Beechwood Books, 1984.

Chapman, Jefferson, <u>Tellico Archaeology,</u> Knoxville: University of Tennessee Press, 1985.

Cromer, Marie, <u>Modern Indians of Alabama,</u> Birmingham: Southern University Press, 1984.

Daniels, Jonathan, <u>The Devil's Backbone-The Story of the Natchez Trace,</u> New York, McGraw-Hill,1962.

Debo, Angie, <u>The Rise and Fall of The Choctaw Republic,</u> Norman: University of Oklahoma Press, 1986.

Dobyns, Henry F., <u>Their Numbers Became Thinned,</u> Knoxville: The University of Tennessee Press, 1983.

Foreman, Grant, <u>Indian Removal,</u> Norman, OK, University of Oklahoma Press, 1986.

Foreman, Grant, <u>The Five Civilized Tribes,</u> Norman: University of Tennessee Press, 1934.

Gentry, Dorothy, <u>Life and Legend of Lawrence County, Alabama,</u> Tuscaloosa: Nottingham-SWS, Inc., 1962.

Gibson, Arrell, <u>The Chickasaws,</u> Norman, OK, University of Oklahoma Press, 1971.

Harris, W. Stuart, <u>Dead Towns of Alabama,</u> University, Alabama: The University Press, 1977.

Hudson, Charles, <u>The Southeastern Indian,</u> Knoxville: University of Tennessee Press, 1976.

Jones, Margaret Jean, <u>Combing Cullman County,</u> Cullman, Alabama: Modernistic Printers, Inc., 1972.

Krebs, W. Phillip, <u>Ten Thousand Years of Alabama Prehistory,</u> Alabama State Museum of Natural History Bulletin 8, 1986.

Leftwich, Nina, <u>Two Hundred Years at Muscle Shoals,</u> Northport: The American Southern Publishing Company, 1935.

Lewis, Thomas M. And Madeline Kneberg, <u>Tribes That Slumber,</u> Knoxville: University Press, 1958.

McDonald, William L., "White Path, The Protector of Indian Lands", <u>Journal of Muscle Shoals History</u>. Tennessee Valley Historical Society, Vol. 5, 1977.

Ortmann, A. E., <u>Science (New Series),</u> Vol. LX No. 1564, December 16, 1924.

Perdue, Theda, <u>Slavery and the Evolution of Cherokee Society,</u> 1540-1866. Knoxville: The University of Tennessee Press; 1979.

Royall, Anne, <u>Letters From Alabama 1817- 1822,</u> University of Alabama Press, 1969.

Satz, Ronald N., <u>Tennessee's Indian Peoples,</u> Knoxville: The University of Tennessee Press, 1979.

Saunders, Col. James Edmond, <u>Early Settlers of Alabama,</u> Easley, S.C.: Southern Historical Press, 1977. Reprint of the 1899 ed. published at New Orleans by L. Graham and Son.

Soday. Frank: J., "Archaeological Field Methods, "<u>Journal of Alabama Archaeology,</u> Vol. 2, Issue 1, 1956.

Steffens, Dr. John E. and Anita Chisholm, <u>Oklahoma's Indian People</u>: <u>Images of Yesterday. Today and Tomorrow,</u> American Indian Institute University of Oklahoma, 1983.

Summersell, Charles Grayson, <u>Alabama History for Schools,</u> Montgomery: Viewpoint Publications, 1981.

Swanton, John R., <u>The Indian Tribes of North America,</u> Smithsonian Institution Press, Bureau of American Ethnology, Bulletin 145. Washington, D.C., 1952.

Swanton, John R., <u>The Indians of the Southeastern United States,</u> Washington: Smithsonian Institution Press, 1987.

Thompson, Wesley S., <u>The Free State of Winston,</u> Winfield, Alabama: Pareil Press, 1968.

Vogel, Joseph O., <u>Nature Notebook,</u> Alabama Museum of Natural History, University, Alabama, 1982.

W.H.G. and Spencer Waters, "Ittaloknah or The Battle of Indian Tomb Hollow- A Story of North Alabama." <u>The Moulton Democrat</u> 1856 and researched by Waters, 1967.

Walthall, John A., <u>Moundville</u>. Alabama Museum of Natural History, University, Alabama, 1977.

Webb, William S., <u>An Archaeological Survey of Wheeler Basin on the Tennessee River in Northern Alabama,</u> Smithsonian Institution Bureau of American Ethnology Bulletin No. 122, 1939.

Picture Index

Word Index

Oklahoma, 88, 132, 134, 141, 197, 198

Old Settlers, 51, 103

Opothleyaholo, 118

Overhill Towns, 99, 189

P

Paleo, 1, 2, 3, 4, 5, 6, 23, 200

Panther, 170, 171, 173, 174, 175, 176, 177, 179, 180, 181, 182, 188

Path Killer, 62, 63, 150

Path Killer Creek, 62

Perry Site, 28

Petroglyphs, 27

pipe, 7, 19, 32, 193

Poarch Band, 141, 142, 143, 145, 146

Polygamy, 90

Pontotoc Treaty, 126

Poplar Log Cove, 5, 194

pottery, 9, 11, 13, 14, 17, 29, 30, 31, 57

Poverty Point, 13

Preston, Greg
  Greg Preston, 138, 201

Prince Madoc, 80, 160, 163

Proclamation Line, 99

R

railroad, 66, 111, 112, 113, 114, 116, 201

Red Bay, Alabama, 2

Red Clay, 115

Red Eagle, 86, 88

Red River, 129

Red Stick, 87

Red Welshmen, 158, 162

Rhea, 58, 104, 105

Riddle, Dollie
  Dollie Riddle, 42, 200

Riddle, Straud
  Straud Riddle, 71

Ridge, 68, 98, 101, 103

Ridge Path, 68, 98

Ridge Road, 68

Riley, Spencer
  Spencer Riley, 151

Rogers, John
  John Rogers, 103

Rogers, Will
  Will Rogers, 149, 158

Rogers, William
  William Rogers, 115

Ross Landing, 116

Ross, John
  John Ross, 151, 158, 201

Royall, Anne
  Anne Royall, 58, 59, 62, 64, 65, 66, 104, 105, 106

Russell County, 46, 124, 194

Russellville, 68

Y

Rickey Butch Walker is a lifelong native son of the Warrior Mountains. He descends from Cherokee, Creek, and Celtic (Scots-Irish) people who migrated into the hills and coves of the mountainous region of north Alabama some 250 years ago. He, as was his father, is a member of the Echota Cherokee Tribe of Alabama. His Indian name is Fish Bird in honor of his fifth, fourth, and third great grandmothers-Catherine Kingfisher, Experience Fish, and Elizabeth Bird.

The kingfisher and fish bird (Osprey) love to fish and so does Butch. In addition, the osprey is of contrasting colors of black and white which identify Butch's character. Things that rule his life are true or false, yes or no, and black or white with virtually no gray areas; therefore, he lives his life somewhat as an open book. Also, according to Indian legend, the birds of prey soar high in the sky and carry the prayers of the earthly creatures to the great spirit. Fish Bird (Butch) has his entire adult life been an advocate to preserve and protect the environment for all the earthly creatures that are unable to speak for themselves.

As a young boy, Butch was born and raised in the shadows of the Warrior Mountains where he was taught by his grandpa the ways of the wild. He squirrel hunted on Brushy Mountain, trapped in Sugar Camp Hollow, searched for ginseng in Indian Tomb Hollow, and fished in West Flint Creek. He walked with his grandparents on old Indian trails including Black Warriors' Path, Sipsie Trail, and many others. He explored the deep canyons, rolling hills, steep bluff lines, and vast hollows containing beautiful waterfalls where he would stand in the spray to cool off on a hot day. He was nourished by the subsistence of West Flint Creek and surrounding hardwood bottoms, and molded from traveling the trails and paths his people once trod. He grew up with a fierce love for the Warrior Mountains in which his ancestors lived, died, and are buried.

In 1966 because of the love of his mountainous homeland, Butch became an advocate to stop the clear cutting of old growth woodlands that he roamed and hunted as a youngster. He worked to help establish the Sipsey Wilderness Area which was dedicated in 1975 and wrote weekly articles about the forest for the Moulton Advertiser. In 1992, Butch teamed up with Lamar Marshall and helped begin the Bankhead Monitor to fight the clear cutting and destructive practices by the United States Forest Service taking place in the sacred Indian Tomb Hollow. The Monitor became Wild Alabama and later Wild South. Butch served as Chairman of the Board of Directors until Wild South merged with the Southern Appalachian Biodiversity Project in 2006.

Rickey Butch Walker retired after some 35 years with the Lawrence County Board of Education during which he earned post graduate degrees in science, education, and supervision. He taught high school science for 11 years and served as Director of Lawrence County Schools' Indian Education Program and Oakville Indian Mounds Education Center until his retirement in 2009. In addition to his Masters Thesis, he has written several books including *High Town Path, Warrior Mountains Folklore, Indians of the Warrior Mountains, Indian Trails of the Warrior Mountains, Warrior Mountains Indian Heritage, Warrior Mountains Indian Heritage Student Edition, Doublehead: Last Chickamauga Chief, Chickasaw Chief George Colbert: His Family and His Country,* and *Appalachian Indians of Warrior Mountains.* Other titles pending publication are *Celtic Indian Boy of Applachia, Black Fold Tales of Appalachia, Soldier's Wife: Cotton Fields to Berlin and Tripoli, Appalachian Indian Trials of the Chickamauga,* and *When Cotton Was King of the South.*

You can find Butch's book at Amazon.com or www.Historicaltruth101.com.

You can also subscribe to his weekly blog at www.RickeyButchWalker.com or

http://rickeybutchwalker.blogspot.com to receive Butch's weekly updates on the historical research he is currently writing.

Bluewater Publications is a multi-faceted publishing company capable of meeting all of your reading and publishing needs. Our two-fold aim is to:

1) Provide the market with educationally enlightening and inspiring research and reading materials.
2) Make the opportunity of being published available to any author and or researcher who desire to be published.

We are passionate about preserving history; whether through the re-publishing of an out-of-print classic, or by publishing the research of historians and genealogists. Bluewater Publications is the *Peoples' Choice Publisher*.

For company information or information about how you can be published through Bluewater Publications, please visit:

www.BluewaterPublications.com

Also check Amazon.com to purchase any of the books that we publish.

Confidently Preserving Our Past,
Bluewater Publications.com

www.ingramcontent.com/pod-product-compliance
Lightning Source LLC
Chambersburg PA
CBHW081358270326
41930CB00015B/3347